# PRODUC

# SUPERCHARGER

## Reach Your Goals Faster by Working More Effectively on the Right Things

## Matthew McClure

I

ISBN 978-1-735-6686-0-4 Paperback

ISBN 978-1-735-6686-1-1 eBook

**Dedication**

This book is dedicated to Elon Musk, one of the most productive people in history.

**Acknowledgments**

Cover design: James Ulysse

# CONTENTS

Interactions with Others

# Introduction

You can always make more money, and if you get sick, you can later regain your health. However, you can't get back any of the time you spend, which makes it your most limited resource.

At the end of their lives, the elderly often state that they feel far more regret about not pursuing their dreams than they do about any actions they took. By achieving a higher level of productivity, you can make much more progress on your most important career and life objectives much faster than you otherwise could. This can help you make the most of your short time here on Earth, so you'll have little to no regret about how you spent your time.

Some days you might find that you're inundated with a barrage of interruptions, distractions, and fire drills that seem to keep you from accomplishing as much as you thought you could even though you worked very hard. At the end of these days, you might realize that you didn't make anywhere near as much progress as you were expecting, which can leave you frustrated, stressed, and overwhelmed.

This book will help you take greater control over your work so you can say goodbye to the days where you know you could have accomplished more.

By increasing your level of productivity, you'll gain a variety of benefits, including:

- More freedom to pursue the most meaningful things in your life
- A lower level of stress and anxiety
- Improved focus
- A feeling that you're better prepared and more organized
- A greater sense of accomplishment

- More leisure time to do the things you want to do
- A greater feeling of control over your work and your life
- A greater ability to perform at a high level, and a greater ability to be compensated accordingly

By achieving a much higher level of productivity, you can also gain others' trust in your ability to get things done well and on time. As you increase your own personal productivity, and that of your team if you have one, over time people will start to notice. They will increasingly realize they can consistently count on you to get critical tasks done well and on time. This can lead to greater opportunities for you to take on more exciting and meaningful work that better matches your skills, interests, and abilities.

## What it Means to Be "Productive"

P roductivity is not about overloading yourself with work and being as busy as you can possibly be. People who work long hours that are frequently stressed and overwhelmed with their work are not necessarily accomplishing more.

Instead, productivity is about reaching your goals faster by working more effectively on the right things. When you spend more of your time working more efficiently on your highest value tasks, you can accomplish more in less time and with less effort. In a nutshell, being productive is about working smarter.

# Chapter 1 – Identify Very Clearly What You Want, and Develop a Plan to Get It

R ather than diving straight into productivity techniques, it's a good idea to start by determining what you want to achieve. This can help you steer your limited time and energy toward the objectives that you care the most about accomplishing. Setting goals is one way to clarify what you want.

However, some people avoid setting goals to evade the feeling of failure if they don't accomplish them. The ironic thing is that by not setting goals at all, these people deny themselves the benefits that come with establishing specific targets to work toward.

If you're not the type of person who is motivated by setting goals, you can instead identify problems you want to solve. Either approach will help you get more of what you want out of life while simultaneously overcoming problems you don't want in your life.

In this chapter, we're going to go over how you can set goals for yourself. When you're working with a clear purpose toward something that matters to you deeply, you'll be more energized to overcome obstacles standing between you and what you want.

One way to come up with goals for yourself is to think about what you want and what you don't want. Think about what types of changes you'd like to see in your work life and your personal life and develop goals to support those changes.

You could also perform a "back from the future" visualization. Imagine it's five years from now, and you've achieved what you want in the most critical areas of your life. This can include goals you reached related to your career, your finances, and your relationships. Write down what each part of your life will look like in explicit detail and what you did over the previous five years to get there. Use this information to help inform which goals you'd want to set for yourself and achieve so you can arrive at that desired future state.

It's also important to realize that if your circumstances change, it might no longer make sense for you to pursue one of your goals. If you come across this scenario, realize that any time, energy, and money you spent pursuing the goal in the past is a sunk cost. Let your previous investment go and focus your resources on achieving your remaining goals.

If you don't develop a plan for how you'll choose your goals and how you'll accomplish them, goal setting runs the risk of being merely wishful thinking. Therefore, we're going to cover how you can use the "SMART" goal-setting process, including setting some big hairy audacious goals to help you with this part of the process.

### Set "SMART" Goals

When you choose your goals, you can use a popular form of goal setting called "SMART." This entails setting goals that are specific, measurable, achievable, relevant, and time-bound.

Set goals that are "specific." Your goals should be well-defined, so you'll know exactly what you're trying to accomplish. One way to perform this step is to use the who, what, when, where, why, and how framework. First, identify who you would work with to achieve the goal, what you would do to achieve the goal, and when you would do the necessary work. Next, determine where you would perform the required work, why you're pursuing this goal, and your overall plan for how you're going to achieve it.

Make sure your goals are "measurable." These measurements

will ideally make it crystal clear whether or not you've accomplished a particular goal. You can also measure specific milestones toward your accomplishment of a goal so you can track your progress along the way.

Choose goals that are "achievable." These goals would be at just the right level of difficulty for you to make a realistic accomplishment. The idea is that you don't want your goals to be so easy that you'd be operating far below your potential. Similarly, it's a good idea to think twice before you set goals where it would be nearly impossible for you to accomplish them. However, as we will discuss in the next section on BHAG goals, it's also a good idea to set some especially audacious goals to achieve your maximum potential.

Review your goals to make sure they're "relevant" to you. When you attach significant meaning to accomplishing your goals, and you have strong reasons for achieving them, it can be easier for you to put in the work necessary to overcome obstacles to achieve them. Therefore, it's crucial that you develop a compelling "why" for each of your goals.

Target goals that are "time-bound." It won't always be possible to have the exact date by which you want to accomplish a goal. However, there are significant benefits to setting a deadline for your achievement of each of your goals. Without a deadline, your goals could take much longer to accomplish, and you might be less likely to accomplish them at all.

## Set "BHAG" Goals as Part of Your Goal Setting Process

I t can also be beneficial to select one or two "BHAGs," which stands for "big, hairy, audacious goals." These are stretch goals that are especially meaningful to you. The significant benefits of accomplishing these goals can inspire you to do the work necessary to achieve them.

In addition to your standard "SMART" goals and your ambitious "BHAG" goals, it can also help you to set one or two smaller goals that are easier to achieve. This can help you build momentum on your way to accomplishing bigger things. These smaller goals could come in the form of breaking down one of your bigger goals into tiny pieces. When you achieve these smaller goals, you'll start to see yourself making more visible progress. This can increase your motivation to put in the work necessary to achieve larger goals.

## Write Your Goals Down, and Use Affirmations and Visualizations

It's important to write down your goals. Committing your goals to paper, or an electronic format of your choice, can increase the likelihood that you'll accomplish them. To keep them top of mind, it can be helpful to continue to write them down periodically until you achieve them, such as once each morning or once a week.

Some people have found affirmations to be a helpful tool to keep them on track to achieve their goals. With an affirmation, you state what you want in the positive as if it's already happened. For example, you can say, "I earn $100,000 per year" instead of saying, "I'm going to earn $100,000 per year eventually."

In addition to affirmations, you can also use visualizations to help you achieve your goals. When you visualize a goal, you close your eyes and imagine yourself working toward it, as well as what it will look like when you achieve what you want to accomplish. This is a technique used by many Olympic athletes. It takes into account that your brain has a difficult time discerning between real events and events you visualize in your mind.

Life would be simpler if the same techniques and strategies worked for everyone, but this is not the case. Some people find that they're less motivated when they focus their mind on already having achieved what they want. This is because they start to feel more relaxed when they see what it would look like to reach the finish line. Therefore, an alternative to affirmations and visualizations is to focus on challenges standing between you and what you want. This approach can help motivate you to want to do the work necessary to overcome those challenges.

Experiment with affirmations, visualizations, and focusing on overcoming your challenges to see which of these strategies helps you the most personally to make significant progress toward achieving your goals. Put considerable thought into choosing the goals you'll pursue, and then "decide" to make them happen. The original root of the word "decide" means "to cut off from" because when you "decide" to do something, you're cutting off the possibility of not doing it.

Overall, by identifying very clearly what you want and developing a plan to make it happen, you can ensure the work you perform will move you closer to the specific results you want to achieve.

# Chapter 2 – Identify and Prioritize Your Highest Value Tasks

S ome of the tasks you perform are much more important to your long-term success and happiness than others. Therefore, the better you are at identifying your highest value tasks and focusing your limited resources on completing them, the more productive you'll be. However, before you can start working on your highest value tasks, you need to have a way to identify which of your tasks would create the most value.

In this chapter, we're going to go over the Eisenhower Methodology and the Pareto Principle, which can help you identify your highest value work. We'll also cover strategies you can use to avoid wasting your time on tasks that wouldn't be a good use of your time and effort.

## The Eisenhower Method

A nother way to prioritize your tasks is to consider their relative importance and urgency. This approach is typically referred to as the Eisenhower Method, which is named after its creator, former U.S. President Dwight D. Eisenhower. This technique is also included in Stephen Covey's "First Things First" methodology.

The Eisenhower Method involves classifying each of your tasks into one of four boxes based on each task's importance and urgency. One of the boxes includes tasks that are both important and urgent. Another box contains tasks that are neither important nor urgent. The remaining two boxes are for tasks that are either important or urgent, but not both. Now let's look at each of these boxes in more detail.

The first box includes tasks that are both urgent and important. An example of this type of task is a key deliverable you need to complete for an important client within the next hour. Your tasks that are both important and urgent should typically be your top priority. However, do what you can to reduce the number of tasks that fall into this box to avoid burning yourself out.

The second box includes tasks that are important but not urgent. An example of this type of task would be an effort to identify and implement improvements to some of your team's processes. It's easy to put off tasks in this box thinking that you'll get to them later because they're not urgent. However, these tasks can produce significant results over the long term. Therefore, spend as much time of your time as possible on tasks in this box.

The third box includes tasks that are urgent but not important. An example of this type of task is a coworker asking for you to help him pick out which ugly sweater he should wear to your company's Ugly Sweater Contest. Many of the tasks in this box are requests you receive from others where they're asking you to help them meet one of their pressing needs. It's easy to feel good when you complete tasks in this box because this type of work frequently involves leveraging your resources to help others. Also, given that many of these tasks are quick and relatively easy to perform, you can get a sense of accomplishment by doing tasks in this box. It's important to be a team player and help others to a certain extent. However, if you spend too much of your time on tasks in this box, it can detract from your ability to get your own work done. You can typically increase your productivity by spending less of your time on these tasks, which are urgent but not important. One way to do this is to be more selective about the help you provide to others for tasks that fall far outside of your primary area of responsibility.

The fourth box includes tasks that are neither important nor urgent. An example of this type of task is checking social media without any particular purpose in mind. These tasks are typically the least valuable you can perform. Therefore, consider reducing how much time you spend on them.

## The Pareto Principle

As you start thinking about the best way to prioritize your tasks, keep in mind the Pareto Principle, which is also commonly known as the "80/20 Rule." This rule states that approximately 80% of your results typically come from only 20% of your efforts. However, you don't have to stop there.

The best way to implement the 80/20 Rule is similar to the way a Russian nesting doll is inside another doll, which itself is inside another doll. When you apply the 80/20 Rule, start by first identifying the 20% of your efforts that produce 80% of your results. Then, take that 20% of your efforts, and determine the 20% of that 20% that accounts for most of your results. You can repeat this process as many times as you'd like until you've identified the relatively few tasks you perform that disproportionately produce the most value.

Then, spend as much of your time as possible on your most valuable tasks while reducing how much time you spend on your least valuable tasks. You can reduce how much time you spend on your least valuable tasks by delegating them to others, reducing the extent of the work you perform on them, or by not completing them at all.

## Think Twice Before Taking on Low-Value Tasks

It's not uncommon to receive an onslaught of requests from a variety of sources throughout the day. Many people say "yes" to most of these requests to portray themselves as a team player or to avoid a potential confrontation they could encounter if they push back on a request.

If people start to notice that you typically say "yes" to almost any request, over time, you might receive more frequent and increasingly bold requests of various kinds. When you're overly responsive to requests, others might start giving you an increasingly large portion of their workload if they find that it's easy to get you to do their work.

Flight attendants typically instruct that if there is a loss of cabin pressure, you should put on your own oxygen mask first before you help others. Likewise, make sure you have enough bandwidth to complete your own work before you spend too much time putting out others' urgent "fires."

You can significantly increase your productivity by resisting the urge to say "yes" to every request for help that you receive. Instead, filter the requests you receive. Over time you can cultivate a stronger ability and willingness to say "no" to tasks that don't make sense for you to perform.

It's tempting to agree to perform tasks when you don't need to do them right away. You might think that next week or next month you'll have more free time than you do today. This could influence you to agree to requests for help that don't require any immediate action. However, there's a good chance that unexpected new things will come up that will make you just as busy in the future as you are right now. Therefore, be especially cautious about agreeing to take on low-value tasks that seem manageable because you wouldn't need to do them right away.

## How to Filter the Requests You Receive

It's important to be responsive to others' requests within reason. However, if you take on every request that anyone would like to give you, you could jeopardize your ability to get your own most important work done. Therefore, it's smart to put others' requests for your help through a filter.

When you receive a request from someone other than your boss, and you're determining if it makes sense for you to help, consider who is making the request. If the person asking for your help has been reasonably responsive to your requests in the past, then it could make sense for you to help them. In contrast, be cautious about going out of your way to assist people who consistently take from others while being highly reluctant to return the favor. Also, consider your company's culture. For example, if you work for an organization where people have thin skin and are easily offended, think twice before significantly pushing back on requests you receive.

If someone asks you to do a task that you don't think needs to be done, share these thoughts with the person asking you to do it to make sure you're not missing something. It's also possible you're not the best person to fulfill a request. If you think it would make more sense for another person or team to handle a request, share this insight with the requester.

**How to Handle Low-Value Tasks You Receive From Your Boss or an Important Client**

If you receive a request from your boss or an important client, be as supportive as possible and think very carefully before pushing back on any aspect of the request. However, if one of these requests would require you to do something that would jeopardize your ability to complete other critical deliverables, seek clarity regarding what you should prioritize. This helps manage expectations while simultaneously making sure you focus your efforts on your highest priority tasks.

If your boss or an important client asks you to perform a low-value task that looks like it doesn't need to be done, think before you start working on it. If you come up with a more streamlined solution, which might involve not performing the task, then you can suggest an alternative approach.

If your boss or an important client asks you to prioritize a task that you believe should have a lower priority, consider sharing this thought diplomatically. For example, you could say something such as,

*"I estimate it will take me approximately two days to complete this new task, so if I prioritize it as my top priority, then critical deliverable X would not be ready until Monday of next week. Therefore, I just wanted to double-check with you to see if you*

*would want me to spend a few more hours to finish critical deliverable X before I get started on this new task."*

## Cultivate an Ability to Decline Extraneous Requests

D eclining to take on certain requests you receive requires a strong backbone and an ability to handle potential confrontations with others, but it's worth it. The alternative of not taking control of your time and letting others unreasonably offload their work onto you can drain your energy, increase your stress, and decrease your ability to get the rest of your work done on time.

Legendary investor Warren Buffett once said,

*"The difference between successful people and really successful people is that really successful people say 'no' to almost everything."*

One way to cultivate a stronger ability to say "no" to requests is to have a clear picture in your mind of your most important goals and what you need to do to achieve them. The more you understand at a deep level that taking on additional tasks could delay your progress toward your most important goals, the easier it will be for you to decline extraneous requests. If you reduce the amount of time and effort you spend on low-value tasks you take on from others, you can increase your productivity by spending more of your time on your own highest value tasks.

## Examples of Ways You Can Politely Decline Extraneous Requests

W hen you decline to take on requests to perform low-value work for others, you don't need to use the word "no." Instead, it's often more effective to choose wording that politely declines the ask. Here are some examples of how you can communicate to others that you don't intend to assist them with their requests.

*"I'm focused on getting a big project done right now. I would help if I had less on my plate, but I'm not able to get involved in this task right now."*

*"For the next several days, I'm going to be focused on getting one of my big projects done, but if you check back with me in about a week, I might be able to help."*

*"My plate is full right now, and that doesn't sound like something I would be able to get to soon. However, you could consider reaching out to John Smith, who might have more bandwidth to help with this."*

## Ways to be More Productive When You Agree to Take on a New Task

When you agree to take on a new task, sometimes you'll receive work requirements that ask for an elaborate amount of work to be performed. Don't do more work than is necessary. In these cases, let the requester know your thoughts on the appropriate level of work and see if that would fulfill the specified need.

Also, when you agree to assist with a new task, realize it's not always necessary for you to drop everything you're doing to start working on it right away. Get clarity on when the work truly needs to be finished rather than the requester's ideal target completion date. This can help you better fit a new task into your existing workload with less of a disruption.

# Chapter 3 – Take Action and Overcome Procrastination to Get What You Want

A fter you determine what you want and what you need to do to get there, start taking consistent action until you achieve your goal. It's important to remember that accomplishing great things is typically more of a marathon than a sprint. Therefore, be careful to avoid burning yourself out.

When I was in high school, during our first invitational cross-country meet, a freshman on my team sprinted ahead of everyone else and was in first place for the first few minutes of the race. However, he never crossed the finished line. When the race was over, we didn't know where he was, so a group of us walked back to see if we could find him. Several minutes later, we found him lying down on a large pile of bark mulch approximately halfway through the course. The lesson from this is that although it might look flashy to start working toward one of your goals with an unsustainably fast sprint, it's generally a better idea to pace yourself and put in the work consistently over time to get what you want.

We're going to start by going over some common procrastination triggers, and along the way, we'll go over tactics you can use to address each one.

## Procrastination Trigger: Difficulty and Complexity

Y ou might tend to procrastinate on tasks that are very difficult and complex, especially if they require significant thought and focused attention to complete.

One way to overcome this procrastination trigger is to work on this type of task during the time of day when you have the most energy and are best able to focus. For many people, this time is first thing in the morning.

Another way you can overcome procrastinating on difficult and complex tasks is to break them into multiple smaller tasks. Shift your focus away from trying to work on one big task, and instead focus on completing smaller pieces of the larger task. For example, if your goal is to develop a spreadsheet that will forecast your company's sales over the next several quarters, break this goal into smaller sub-steps. In this example, one of the smaller sub-steps might be for you to identify and obtain the data necessary to perform the analysis.

### Procrastination Trigger: Confusion Over Next Steps and an Unclear Desired End Result

One of the most common procrastination triggers is a lack of clarity regarding the specific next step you'd need to take to make progress on a task. A related trigger is a lack of clarity regarding what the desired end result will look like. When you don't have a clear picture of where you're going, it can be harder to get started.

To overcome this trigger, perform the groundwork necessary to clarify what you want to see in the finished product. Perform this work on your own if you can, but you can also leverage others' knowledge and expertise. This could include conversations with your boss, colleagues, a mentor, or someone on another team who might have performed similar work in the past. If you don't have anyone at your company or in your network who would be able to help, there are other resources you can leverage, such as Google, YouTube, or Quora. If you look to others outside of your company for help, it's important to make sure you don't share any proprietary or confidential information.

In addition to clarifying what you'd like to see in the finished product, it can also be helpful to develop more clarity on what your intermediate work product will look like at various stages of completion along the way. This could involve making a list of the things you need to do to complete the task. If you break this list down and organize it, you should be able to come up with the next steps you would need to take. This can help you more clearly identify where to start.

## Procrastination Trigger: Input Needed from Others

S ome of your tasks might require input from others before you can complete them. It can be easy to procrastinate on these types of tasks by clinging to the fact that you need things from others to make progress on your work. For this type of task, identify what you can do to move forward. This might include working on aspects of the task for which you don't need others' inputs. Also, it could involve setting up reminders to check in with the person you're waiting on to see if there's anything you can do that will help them provide the input faster.

If the person is taking too long to provide you with the requested deliverable, consider your alternatives. This could include asking someone else to provide you with the deliverable, producing the deliverable yourself, or even doing without the deliverable if it's not truly necessary.

## Procrastination Trigger: Undesirability

Y ou might procrastinate on a task if it's unpleasant. Tasks can be unpleasant for a variety of reasons, including tasks you view as boring and tasks where the raw inputs you need to leverage are extremely disorganized.

To get yourself to overcome this obstacle, start by identifying what aspects of a task are undesirable to you, and then adjust your approach to completing it until the task becomes more tolerable for you to perform. Work to find a meaning you can latch onto even if it's not clear right away. Use this meaning to clarify for yourself why you must complete the task, including the negative implications of not completing it.

You might consider organizing a file cabinet to be an undesirable and tedious task. However, it can be helpful to generate meaning even for mundane tasks such as this. For example, you could come up with a scenario in which you're looking forward to leaving the office at the end of a particular day to go on a vacation. A few minutes before you were about to turn off your computer, your boss sends you an urgent message that you need to locate a specific file. By having the file cabinet organized, you can simply take a couple of minutes to pull the file and provide it to your boss before you head out the door for your vacation. In this example, by connecting the mundane task of organizing a file cabinet with a scenario in which it could help you avoid a delay in an upcoming vacation, you can make it more meaningful to you.

Depending on how undesirable a task is, you might need to be creative to come up with a compelling "why" regarding the task's deeper meaning. However, once you have a better reason for completing a task, it could be much easier for you to overcome an urge to procrastinate on it.

Another way to get yourself to avoid procrastinating on especially undesirable tasks is to make a conscious decision about the specific thing you'll work on first. This can help you feel like you have more control over the task, and it can help you get some initial momentum toward completing it.

Using the example above of the relatively undesirable task of organizing a file cabinet, you could get started by choosing one specific area where you'll begin. For instance, you could start by setting up an index file in Excel that will list out each of the files along with their location in the file cabinet. Alternatively, you could take even more control over the task by seeing if you could instead digitize the entire contents of the file cabinet so the files could be searchable and accessible from any computer. By exerting more control over the process and starting by working on an item of your choice, it can be easier to get yourself to overcome procrastination and accomplish the tasks you need to complete.

## Procrastination Trigger: Perfectionism

A t times you might find yourself avoiding a task until conditions are perfect and you're in a better place to take action. Alternatively, although you might have already made significant progress on a project, you might find it challenging to put your pencil down and stop working on it because you want it to be perfect. If either of these thought processes sounds familiar to you, you might have experienced procrastination related to perfectionism.

It can be attractive to strive for perfectionism because you might care deeply about wanting to produce the best quality work possible. Also, perfectionism is attractive because the more you tweak a final work product before you submit it, the less likely it is that you would receive criticism regarding any imperfections it contains. However, these benefits come at a cost.

The act of striving for perfection is the opposite of the Pareto Principle. The amount of incremental work required to make something that is great even better is typically exponentially higher than the resulting improvement in quality. We often spend far longer than we need to when we complete tasks to make sure our output is as close to perfect as possible. If you're part of a team manufacturing a part for the International Space Station, then maybe perfection could be critically important. However, although perfection might seem like a noble objective, it's rare for it to be necessary or even desirable.

Therefore, consider whether the task you're working on truly needs to be perfect and then allocate your time accordingly. For example, if you don't re-read your email to a colleague three times before you hit send, and as a result, you use the word "its" without an apostrophe instead of "it's" with an apostrophe, realize that it's not going to be the end of the world.

The latest iPhone is far better than the original iPhone. However, Apple still came out with the first iPhone knowing that they could have taken more time to incorporate additional enhancements. Similarly, by focusing on getting something done rather than obsessing over making it perfect, you can increase your ability to complete a greater amount of high-quality work rather than having many partially completed projects.

Another strategy to overcome perfectionism is to complete your first draft of a task knowing you'll come back and review it later. At first, don't worry about whether what you're putting together is perfectly polished. Then, once you've completed your first draft, come back to review it and make any necessary edits. This approach can give you far better results as compared to moving at a slow pace as you try to produce perfect work the first time.

Parkinson's Law states that the time a task takes to complete expands to the amount of time available to complete it. One way to overcome this obstacle is to set deadlines for completing specific tasks you want to accomplish, which can help you put your pencil down and overcome perfectionism.

To the extent that it makes sense for your specific line of work, consider leveraging the startup concept of "minimum viable product" (MVP). Identify the smallest amount of work you can do that will substantially achieve the intended objective, and then use that as your target. This can help you develop a working prototype more quickly, which can help you get feedback that can make your next iteration much better.

When it comes to addressing a tendency toward perfectionism, there are two useful sayings you can apply to your workflow that can help you increase your productivity. The first is that "perfect is the enemy of the good," which emphasizes that trying to make your work perfect can come at the expense of not getting a significant amount of good work done. The second saying is that "done is better than perfect." This emphasizes that it's often better to complete high-quality work quickly rather than trying to expend a tremendous amount of time and effort to try to be perfect in everything you do.

Overall, perfectionism typically results in a significant

amount of time and effort being spent to make relatively small improvements in a final work product. Although it can be rare, there are times when absolutely perfect work is required. However, you might be able to accomplish considerably more if you instead calibrate the level of perfection in your work to the amount needed for each particular deliverable. By discontinuing an attempt at perfectionism in everything you do, you can free up a significant amount of time and effort that you could instead use to make significant progress in other areas.

### Procrastination Trigger: Fear of Failure

Sometimes procrastination is fueled by fear, whether conscious or unconscious, that you might not be able to complete a particular task.

To combat this fear, you can view failure as a form of learning. Rather than brushing aside and forgetting about any setbacks you encounter, you can instead analyze the underlying reasons why you didn't succeed. The more you learn from your failures, the better equipped you'll be to overcome similar challenges in the future. Many of the most successful people identify learning from their past failures as an essential stepping stone to their success. Don't give up on a new goal just because your first few steps toward achieving it didn't go as you were expecting.

It can be helpful to set yourself up for small wins early on by focusing on making steady, incremental progress. Then, once you pick up momentum, you can set your sights higher for what you want to achieve.

Another way to overcome a fear of failure is to identify the most likely ways you could fail and then put in safeguards to reduce their likelihood. This will give you peace of mind knowing that even if things don't go exactly according to plan, you've minimized your overall risk of failure.

### Procrastination Trigger: Low Energy

Y ou might have a low level of energy, which could be making it more difficult for you to take the necessary actions to complete a task. Many different factors can contribute to a low level of energy, including inadequate sleep, a food-based energy crash, or a lack of exercise. Negative emotions and limiting beliefs can also contribute to a lower level of energy.

To get yourself out of a rut, make a list of tasks that you find exciting and energizing. If you feel you're less focused, consider taking a break and spending a few minutes on an activity you know will make you feel refreshed and rejuvenated. This could include going for a quick walk, playing with your dog, or getting a drink of water.

There are many fitness tracking apps and devices that can help you better monitor your sleep and diet. Logging the food you eat, especially if your energy is low, can help pinpoint any sensitivities you might have to a particular food. Therefore, consider wearing a fitness tracking device, which can encourage you to be more active, hydrate yourself, and get better sleep.

Significant negative emotions can contribute to a low level of energy, such as anger, disgust, guilt, fear, shame, sadness, or loneliness. Where appropriate, consider talking with a professional counselor or therapist who can help you process and work through these emotions.

If you have a limiting belief that you're the type of person who continually has a low level of energy and that this is just who you are, consider revisiting that assumption. Even if you've had a low level of energy in the past, this doesn't necessarily mean you'll always have a low level of energy in the future. Have an open mind about your ability to make adjustments to your lifestyle that could increase your level of energy going forward.

## Other Strategies for Overcoming Procrastination

C onsider putting some of your money at risk of being donated to a charity whose mission is repulsive to you using a service such as stickK. If you don't follow through on a commitment you make using this tool, stickK will display your name publicly for all to see.

Realize that for some tasks, the more you put them off, the more difficult it will be to accomplish them. If you think deeply about how much more difficult it would be to perform a task in the future, you could be more motivated to start taking action to get it done sooner rather than later.

You could also use social accountability to overcome procrastination. For example, you could tell a few of the people closest to you the date by which you're committed to completing a task. This can increase your motivation to complete the task by that date to be consistent with this commitment. You could also share your goals online with social groups that have similar motivations.

Remember, it's a good idea to eliminate or defer low-value tasks that you don't need to complete right away, if at all. Although it might feel like you're making progress when you spend your time on these items of lower importance, you'd make much more progress by focusing your efforts on any higher-value tasks you've been putting off.

## Raise the Stakes for Continuing to Procrastinate

Take a step back and think about what your life could start to look like in a few years if you keep procrastinating, not just on the task at hand but on future tasks as well. Think about how this could lead to you fretting and stressing over these tasks longer than you need to as a result of delaying getting them done. Also, think about the lack of progress you'd make in your career if your procrastination continues and gets worse.

Then, imagine the opposite. Consider how much more productive you'd be and how much more progress you'd make in your career if you instead start consistently doing what you need to do when you need to do it, whether you feel like it or not.

By looking at things from this perspective, you can better understand the magnitude of the long-term effects of procrastinating. This can help you get more leverage on yourself to stop procrastinating and to start doing what you know you need to do.

Realize it's likely you'll feel the same way tomorrow about completing a task as you do today. This thought process could help you realize it's worth it to overcome the procrastination hurdle you're facing to complete this task as soon as possible.

Also, you can focus on the benefits others will receive if you overcome procrastination and complete a task you've been delaying. Depending on your personality, you might find it to be more motivating to focus on how completing tasks you've been procrastinating on will benefit others you care about more than focusing on the benefits you'd receive yourself.

# Chapter 4 – Clear Your Mind and Build Your Body for Increased Productivity

If you experience burnout from too much stress and not enough rest and rejuvenation, you could experience a significant reduction in your productivity. However, if you make a conscious effort to recharge your batteries periodically rather than trying to work nonstop, you'll have a stronger ability to generate sustained high performance over the long term.

A "work hard, play hard" mindset can help you improve your productivity if you apply it in the right way. For the "work hard" part, you need to be fully engaged and focused on your work. Similarly, when you "play hard," you want to focus exclusively on relaxing and enjoying yourself. This helps you alternate between doing impactful work and recharging your batteries fully so you can be more productive in the future.

In this chapter, we're going to go over things you can do during your non-working time that can significantly increase your productivity.

## Write Down What's on Your Mind

One way to clear your mind is to write down everything that's currently on your mind, which might include things you're trying to remember to do, things you're waiting to receive from other people, and concerns that are on your mind. Simply writing down what's on your mind can be very therapeutic. Once you write down what's on your mind, you can then intelligently choose which of these items you're going to take action on and what the next steps are going to be. Also, perhaps more importantly, you'll be able to identify the things that have been on your mind that you're going to figuratively "let go."

## Meditate

M editating can clear your mind and help you improve your ability to focus. By focusing on your breathing, meditation can supercharge your pre-frontal cortex and reduce the weight of signals you receive from your more primitive limbic system. This can help you make more rational decisions rather than making decisions based excessively on emotion.

When you're ready to meditate, sit down in a comfortable position, and focus on breathing in through your nose and out through your mouth. Your eyes can be open or closed, depending on your preference. Then you can focus on your breath as you breathe in and out. One popular form of meditation is the "box" breathing technique used by U.S. Navy Seals. This involves breathing in for four seconds, holding in the air for four seconds, breathing out for four seconds, and then pausing with your lungs empty of air for four seconds.

Invariably, thoughts will come into your mind as you meditate. When these thoughts come up for you realize that this is normal. Rather than trying to pretend that these extraneous thoughts don't exist, it's generally more effective to acknowledge mentally that an extraneous thought has come up. Next, mentally accept that you're going to let that thought go and then focus back on your breath. Meditating for even a short amount of time each day can have a positive impact on your productivity.

## Be Present

T o be more present, focus on what you're doing while you're doing it. It's normal for your mind to wander, and when it does, acknowledge that it happened and bring your attention back to what you're doing.

Being more present can help you avoid the energy drain associated with stressing about things in your personal life when you're working and vice versa.

### Practice Gratitude

Once a day, write down a few things you're grateful for. You can do this as soon as you get up, right before you go to bed, or at another time of your choosing. This can be especially powerful if you do it toward the end of your day because it can put you in a more relaxed state of mind before you go to sleep.

This helps shift the focus of the reticular activating system in your brain to the good things that happen to you throughout your day, which can make you happier and more productive.

### Close Open Thought Loops

The Zeigarnik Effect states that you have a stronger tendency to remember open loops, such as tasks you're still working on, than you are to remember closed loops, such as tasks you've already completed. Until you either complete a task or choose a clear next step for how you'll address it, the task can detract from your ability to focus because you'll know in the back of your mind that you need to take action on it.

Therefore, it can be useful to write down any concerns that are on your mind as soon as you think about them for the first time. This helps your mind "let go" of these items because you know you'll revisit them at some point in the near future. You don't have to complete a task to get it off your mind. Instead, you only need to know that you have a plan in place to take the appropriate action as necessary in the future.

Then, later when you have time, such as once a week, go through your list of concerns. For each item on the list, identify which items are not within your control. For items that are not within your control, realize that you could handle it even if the worst-case scenario happened, and be at peace with it. For the items that are within your control, determine which items you'll work on over the next week and which ones you're going to defer to a subsequent week.

### Minimize Your Interactions with Negative People

T here's truth to the saying that over time you become more similar to the five people you're the closest to in life. Therefore, only surround yourself with people who are positive and who support you and what you want in life.

## Avoid Venting

E xcessive venting can be destructive because it involves focusing your attention on the negative and does not typically do much to solve problems. Limit the amount of complaining and venting you do to the bare minimum and instead focus on the positive. What you focus on grows in your life.

If you must complain, focus more on what you would like to see in the future and less on what went wrong in the past.

## Ask Yourself Empowering Questions

A big part of life is how you perceive what happens, and there's more than one way to look at things. It can be helpful to periodically ask yourself empowering questions that can get you to focus on the good things and opportunities in your life, which you might otherwise miss if you're focused on the negative.

Here are some examples of empowering questions you can ask yourself:

*"What was the worst thing that happened in my life over the last week, month, or year, and how can I leverage this to create something positive in my life going forward?"*

*"What significant achievements am I going to accomplish over the next week, month or year?"*

*"In what ways am I in an excellent position to achieve the key things I want to accomplish on or ahead of schedule?"*

## Adjust Your View of the Attractiveness of Certain Activities

T o be highly productive, at times you'll need to do things you don't feel like doing. At other times, you'll need to avoid doing things you want to do. However, it can take significant willpower to overcome your desire to do what you feel like doing. One way to overcome this challenge is to shift your view of the desirability of certain activities.

For a task you need to do but don't feel like doing, think deeply about how doing it isn't as bad as you're making it out to be. Find some silver lining in the activity, which might include the benefits of completing the task or the pain you'll experience if you delay completing the task. Similarly, for things you're trying to avoid doing, shift your view of the task to make it as unattractive as possible to reduce your desire to do it.

This approach can increase your ability to do the things you need to do and to avoid doing the things you're trying to avoid doing.

## Take Rejuvenating Vacations

U nplugging from work and taking well-deserved vacations can help revitalize you and increase your overall sense of wellbeing. However, what you do and when you do it when you're on vacation can significantly impact your ability to be productive when you return to work. For example, there's a significant difference between traveling and taking vacations even though most trips for pleasure include an element of each.

Traveling refers more specifically to performing significant activities, such as going on a safari, volunteering at an orphanage, or hiking Mount Kilimanjaro. The days you spend traveling can be some of the most meaningful of your life, and I encourage you to travel extensively. However, personal trips that only include traveling activities don't recharge your batteries as much as trips where you incorporate some vacationing. If your entire trip consists of traveling, you could return to work feeling like you need a vacation from your vacation.

Vacationing refers more specifically to the time you spend resting and relaxing. This could include laying in a hammock on the beach, getting a massage, or sleeping in and ordering room service. Some activities could fall into either the traveling or vacationing category, depending on how relaxing you find them to be, such as jet skiing, four-wheeling, and scuba diving.

Incorporate more traveling elements into the middle of your trip and vacationing elements at the beginning and end of your trip. This can help you recharge your batteries as the trip starts, generate amazing memories from traveling in the middle of your trip, and then rest up toward the end of your trip before you get ready to return to work.

It's better to include activities at the beginning and the end of your trip that you personally find to be relaxing rather than feeling like you need to do any particular set of things. It's your vacation, so customize it however you would like so that it meets your personal preferences as much as possible.

Plan your vacations well in advance so you can have time to look forward to them. A significant part of the happiness and enjoyment associated with doing something fun is the anticipation leading up to the event itself.

When you take a vacation, to the extent possible unplug and disconnect from your work. This is not always possible. If it's impossible for you to completely disconnect from the office during your time off from work, see if you can at least limit your work to specific blocks of time during the day, such as one hour in the morning, one hour in the afternoon, and one hour in the evening. This way, you won't be wasting away the enjoyment of your trip while you check your work email every 15 minutes all day every day.

Let your team know about your upcoming vacations in advance so you can better coordinate work with them before you go on your trip. It can help you enjoy your vacation more if you put in extra work at the office in the few days before you leave on your trip and after you return from your trip. This enables you to start your trip knowing that you're leaving things in a great spot for your team. The extra work you perform when you return to the office helps give you significant momentum at work after you return.

Especially if you're an overachiever, you might feel guilty when you take more than a short amount of time to relax. Doing no work at all for even a couple of days in a row could be unthinkable to you. If this is the case for you, just realize that even spending one restful day a month where you don't work at all will likely result in you being able to think more clearly and get more high-quality work done than if you avoid taking any time off.

Not everyone has the financial resources to trot around the globe. Even if you're on a limited budget right now, there are still things you can do to increase the relaxation and restfulness you experience when you take a vacation. Here are some ideas for rejuvenating things you can do on a vacation day if you're on a constrained budget:

- Take a long walk through a park or go for a hike on a nature trail.

- See a movie or two at the movie theater.

- Go to the best ice cream parlor in your town and order the best combination of ice cream and toppings you can devise.

- Visit a local park and have fun playing on the swings like you're a kid again.

When you return from your vacation, avoid arriving at home late at night when you need to return to work early the next morning. If you can't avoid a flight that will arrive late at night, then take the next day off as a buffer day rather than returning to work immediately. This helps you avoid an abrupt end to your vacation, which can help make your overall vacation experience more relaxing and enjoyable.

**Eat Well**

S imilar to the adage "garbage in, garbage out," if you eat junk food, you'll be more likely to have a low level of energy that could result in you producing more junk work.

One of the easiest and most effective ways to enhance your body's performance for maximum productivity is to stay well hydrated. When you wake up in the morning, your body is typically dehydrated, so having a bottle of water readily available, such as next to your bed or on your bathroom sink, is ideal. Drinking one liter of water shortly after you get up is a great way to kickstart your body. Consider infusing your water with lemons, limes, or mint, which could help you get more excited about drinking it. Experiment with different types of water as much as you need to until you arrive at one that you're able to get yourself to drink consistently every day. Staying hydrated throughout the day is also important. Placing water bottles in a place where you're likely to spend your time can encourage you to drink from them more frequently. You could use a metal water bottle, such as those sold by Yeti and RTIC, that can keep your water cool all day.

In addition to hydrating yourself first thing in the morning and staying hydrated throughout the day, it's also important to have a healthy meal for breakfast. This can set you up for success later in the day. If you start your day by skipping breakfast, or if you eat unhealthy food for breakfast, it can be easier to give in to the temptation to eat unhealthy food later. However, if you build momentum with a healthy breakfast to start your day, it can be easier for you to stay on track and continue to eat well. If you get off track with your eating, acknowledge that you got off track and immediately work to get back on track rather than giving up on eating well altogether.

If you eat certain types of highly processed foods, including foods with a large amount of sugar, you might experience a noticeable reduction in your energy level about an hour after you eat. Avoiding sugar can be especially difficult because it's in so many foods. However, if you can cut back on highly processed foods that reduce your level of energy and replace these foods with more whole foods, such as fresh fruits, vegetables, and fish, you could experience a more consistent level of energy throughout the day.

Everyone reacts differently to food. Taking an at-home food sensitivity test can provide you with insights regarding your immune system's response to a variety of foods. This can help you more quickly pinpoint which foods could be draining your energy and which foods could help you feel more energized. Many physicians can give you a food sensitivity test. Also, there are some companies, such as EverlyWell, that sell at-home food sensitivity tests you can buy online.

Consider keeping healthy snacks with you throughout the day so you can easily eat well if you get hungry in between meals. This can help you avoid the temptation of less healthy options. However, as mentioned above, make sure you're drinking an adequate amount of water throughout the day to stay hydrated. Sometimes you might start to feel hungry when, in reality, your body just needs some additional hydration.

When it comes to food, don't just think about the near-term feelings that come from eating something delicious. Instead, shift your focus to the intermediate- and longer-term effects. For example, if you eat a donut loaded with sugar, the effects you experience in the short term can be very different from those you experience in the long term. When you eat the donut, in the short term, you'll get to taste something delicious. In the intermediate-term, you could become much more tired than you otherwise would have been as you crash down off the sugar high from the donut. In the longer term, you could start to gain a noticeable amount of weight if you eat too many delicious snacks like donuts. Over the very long term, you could experience health complications sooner and more severely if you have an unhealthy lifestyle that prioritizes delicious food over your health.

If it helps, you can think of unhealthy snacks as thieves lurking in the shadows waiting to steal your energy an hour after you eat them or as assassins plotting to kill you off before it's your time to go. Although these mind tricks might sound silly, test them out to see if they help you shift your mindset and habits to eat more of the types of food that will give you a high level of sustained energy.

### Get Your Food Faster and with Less Effort

One evening you might want to go out to eat at a restaurant that has healthy food you love, but you might have second thoughts if the restaurant is busy and you don't have a reservation. One way you can overcome this challenge is to consider eating in the bar area where you can usually seat yourself right away at a high-top table or at the bar area itself.

Also, during the workday, consider going to lunch a little earlier or a little later than everyone else to avoid the lines. Alternatively, consider bringing your lunch to work to avoid those lines altogether. If you do wait in line, consider bringing headphones with you so you can do something productive while you wait, such as listening to an audiobook or podcast.

If you live in an area with many restaurants, you can put together a list of your favorite ones along with your own personal rating regarding the availability of healthy food selections at each restaurant. You can also make a note of when each of these restaurants is open. This way, when you're done with work for the day and want to go out to eat, it can be much easier for you to find a great restaurant with healthy food you'd be happy to eat.

If you cook food at home regularly, consider using a service such as Blue Apron, Plated, or HelloFresh to save yourself some time in acquiring the raw materials you need for your meal preparation. If you don't like to spend much time preparing your food, you could use a service such as Freshly or Factor 75, which send you ready to eat meals that you only need to heat before you eat them.

Also, if you're in the zone working and don't want to interrupt your progress to pick up some food, consider using a meal delivery service such as Uber Eats, DoorDash, or GrubHub.

**Exercise**

B illionaire Sir Richard Branson attributed his high level of productivity to staying fit. In a blog post, Branson stated,

*"The only reason I'm able to do all the things I do and to keep on top of a busy schedule without getting too stressed is because I stay fit."*

In a video interview posted to the FourHourBodyPress channel on YouTube, Joe Polish asked Branson,

*"What are your thoughts on being productive as it relates to health, fitness, and working out?"*

In his response, Branson stated,

*"I definitely can achieve twice as much in a day by keeping fit."*

Staying fit, both mentally and physically, is no guarantee you'll also become a billionaire. However, it can help you increase your level of energy, your ability to focus, and your productivity. Exercise can give you more energy, which helps you increase your ability to work with high intensity for extended periods of time. Exercising is also a great way to relieve stress as it releases endorphins that increase your overall sense of wellbeing.

If you're able to get yourself to start exercising, that's great. However, if you know yourself well enough that you don't foresee yourself starting to work out as much as you'd like, consider hiring a personal trainer. A personal trainer can help you get started with a workout routine that's customized to your personal needs, such as increasing your level of energy, losing weight, or building muscle mass. Even a few sessions can give you significant momentum toward starting a consistent and personalized workout routine that works for you. If you don't have the money for a personal trainer, consider finding a workout buddy instead. Going to the gym with someone else regularly can increase your desire to work out because you know the other person will be counting on you to be there.

Even if you don't see yourself implementing a rigorous exercise regimen, there are other ways you can start increasing your level of activity, which can boost your productivity. You can take walks around your neighborhood before or after work, or you can go for a walk near your office during lunchtime. Depending on what you focus on during a walk, you can use this time to relax, clear your mind, or come up with creative ideas or solutions to problems. To the extent that you can, try to take your walks in an atmosphere that you find to be relaxing. This could include walking through a park, along a river, or around a lake. However, depending on your personality, you might be the most relaxed walking around a city. Experiment and do what works best for you.

## Get the Right Amount of Quality Sleep and Fall Asleep More Quickly

There are many productivity disadvantages associated with not getting enough high-quality sleep, including irritability, impaired memory, and challenges thinking clearly and concentrating. Alternatively, getting adequate sleep can help you complete tasks that are especially challenging, complex, or that require focused attention.

It's a good idea to avoid eating food a few hours before you go to sleep to give your body time to digest what you eat before you go to sleep. Also, avoid drinking too much liquid a couple of hours before you go to bed to avoid having to get up in the middle of the night to go to the bathroom.

Drinking alcohol before bed can help you get to sleep faster. However, a drawback is that this can cause a substantial reduction in the quality of your sleep. Therefore, to increase the quality of your sleep, avoid drinking alcohol shortly before you go to bed.

Blue light can keep your body from producing as much melatonin as you otherwise would. Since melatonin helps you fall asleep, consider avoiding blue lights emitted by TVs, smartphones, and other electronics for the last hour or two before you go to bed. Some smartphones and tablets have a setting where you can significantly reduce the blue light emitted. If you're especially serious about getting a great night of sleep on a particular night, you can wear glasses that block blue light in the hour or two before you go to bed. These glasses generally have yellow lenses.

If you're in a pinch and you need to fall asleep quickly on a particular night, consider taking some melatonin. However, be cautious about taking melatonin regularly because your body can become somewhat desensitized to it if you take it too often.

If your schedule allows for it, you could establish a routine where you go to bed and wake up at the same time each day. This can help you get to sleep more quickly, and it can also improve the quality of your sleep. Before you go to bed, try taking a cold shower because the cold water could make you feel sleepy more quickly. A noise machine that produces white, pink, or brown noise can block out sounds that might otherwise disturb your sleep, allowing you to fall asleep quicker as well. Also, some people find they can more quickly get to sleep and stay asleep by making it as dark as possible using blackout curtains and a sleep mask, such as those sold by Manta.

Writing down what you're grateful for can help you get into a more relaxed state of mind that is more conducive to going to sleep. Even if you don't write anything down, you could still get some value from thinking of a few things you're grateful for that took place on that day. Also, you could write down any significant concerns on your mind that might prevent you from sleeping. Writing down your concerns can help you get them off your mind.

Especially if you've had a relatively high level of stress earlier in the day, consider taking a few minutes to meditate before you go to bed. Some fitness tracker devices have a feature that helps you with your breathing for this type of short meditation session. Meditating before bed can help you relax, which can help you get to sleep more easily. As part of this meditation, you can do deep breathing where you breathe in for half the amount of time that you breathe out. Perform this deep breathing with your diaphragm rather than with your chest. To determine if you're breathing with your diaphragm, notice if your belly moves in and out when you breathe. The more your belly is moving in and out, the more diaphragmatic breathing you're performing.

While you're lying down in bed with your eyes closed, mentally contract and then relax each of the muscles in your body. Start with your toes and move up to the top of your body. This can give you the final level of relaxation you need to fall asleep quickly.

### Use a Fitness Tracker

Consider using a fitness tracking device, such as those offered by Apple, Fitbit, and Oura, which can help you monitor and manage your physical activity. Although these trackers can help you be more informed about your health, consult a licensed physician before beginning any new exercise or nutrition program.

# Chapter 5 – Use Your Willpower Intelligently to Establish Effective Habits

H ave you ever realized you should do something, but then you ended up not doing it because you didn't feel like it? For many people, this happens every day. In this chapter, we're going to go over some ways you can make this type of situation a less frequent occurrence in your life.

An example of a disconnect between knowledge and action relates to health and fitness. Most people are familiar with the types of things they would need to do to get into much better shape, such as eating healthier food, exercising more, and getting higher-quality rest. They know that consuming a green drink with organic spinach, apples, and other vegetables could be healthier than eating a few donuts. However, even with this knowledge, it's not uncommon for people to choose the donuts over the green drink. Just knowing what you need to do isn't enough. To achieve a high and sustained level of productivity, you need to be able to get yourself to do things you need to do even when you don't feel like doing them.

There's a hard way and an easy way to get yourself to do something you don't want to do. The hard way is to use your limited amount of willpower to exercise self-control. This is a common approach, which is one of the reasons why many people find it so difficult to do what they need to do. Rather than doing things the hard way, a much easier and more effective approach is to use your limited amount of willpower to establish habits. Once you build a habit to do something, it becomes automatic, and you don't have to put in as much thought or expend much willpower to do it.

Before we go any further, let's clarify what we mean by willpower and how you can use it to create habits that will enable you to get yourself to do what you need to do when you need to do it. Willpower is the amount of mental strength you have to tackle the challenges that arise as you go through your day. For example, you use willpower when you make decisions that require significant thought. You also use willpower when you exercise restraint to avoid doing something very tempting, such as turning down a cupcake because you're trying to eat healthier food.

At the beginning of each day, we wake up with a certain amount of willpower, which gets depleted throughout the day as we use it to make decisions and to exert self-control. Psychologists refer to this as ego depletion. Today there are differing viewpoints among experts in the field of psychology regarding ego depletion. For example, Stanford psychologist Carol Dweck and her colleagues found that signs of ego depletion tend to show up primarily in people who believe willpower is a limited resource. Therefore, you might be able to power through your workload if you can convince yourself that willpower is not a limited resource. However, in case this doesn't work for you, we're going to go over some ways you can overcome situations where you feel a lack of willpower to do what you know you need to do.

You can address a shortage of willpower by both increasing your willpower and also by decreasing your willpower depletion. To increase your willpower "muscle," make a conscious effort to do what you need to do when you need to do it, especially when you don't feel like doing it. As your willpower "muscle" gets stronger, you'll find that your "starting" level of willpower each day will be higher. To reduce the depletion of your willpower, you can consciously identify things that reduce your energy and then take steps to eliminate or minimize their impact.

By the time you've expended virtually all your willpower for a particular day, it can be challenging to get yourself to do things you don't want to do. Therefore, avoid wasting your willpower on things that don't matter.

## Avoid Unnecessarily Draining Your Willpower

One of the largest uses of your willpower is decision making. The more you can eliminate or reduce the impact of making unimportant decisions, the more willpower you'll have to use for areas of greater importance in your life. For example, in the morning, you might start the day by deciding what to wear. When you get to work, you might start by deciding what you should work on first. When it gets to be lunchtime, you might take time to decide what you're going to do for lunch.

The more decisions you make, and especially the more thought intensive these decisions are, the more you reduce your willpower. One way to minimize the willpower drain you experience is to make decisions in advance where possible. Each day before you leave work, you can decide what you're going to work on first thing the next morning, which eliminates the need to make this decision when you get to work. By making decisions in advance, you reduce the drain on your willpower that would otherwise occur.

Another way to reduce your willpower is to be more decisive. Consider making decisions more quickly when the different options would have little impact. This will allow you to move on and focus more of your effort and energy on things of higher importance.

When you multitask, which is just rapid task switching, you incur task-switching costs that can drain your willpower. Therefore, reduce your multitasking, especially on tasks that require focused concentration, to help conserve your willpower.

Removing and reducing temptations can also help you conserve your willpower. If you make it easier for yourself to avoid a specific temptation, you don't need to spend as much willpower resisting it. For example, if your cell phone is off and located in the bottom drawer of your desk, it will be less enticing for you to check it while you're working. In this example, by placing your phone out of reach, you can reduce the amount of willpower it takes to avoid picking it up and looking at it while you work.

### Build Habits to Be More Productive

One of the best uses of your limited willpower is the formation of habits. Habits can help you be more consistent in doing what you need to do, even when challenges arise. They can also help you reduce the amount of willpower it takes for you to make consistent progress toward achieving your goals. Further, removing or adjusting any bad habits you might have right now can give you a greater sense of control over your life and help you to be more productive.

Habits are the key to getting yourself to do what you know you need to do when you need to do it, even when you don't feel like doing it. When you build a new habit, you can set it up in such a way that it's inevitable that you'll achieve your goals. For example, if you want to get in the habit of working out every morning, make the necessary adjustments so it's inevitable that you'll work out in the morning. This could involve setting an alarm at night to remind you to go to bed early, putting your workout clothes next to your bed, and starting with a reasonable workout that's not so intense that you'd try to avoid doing it.

Another benefit of establishing effective habits is that they can help you conserve your limited amount of willpower. For example, at first, you might find it to be challenging to get yourself to work out a few times a week. Each time you go to work out, it might take a significant amount of willpower. However, after you make working out a habit, you might find that you actually enjoy working out, and from then on, it might take little, if any, willpower to continue working out.

In addition to establishing new habits that will help you to be more productive, it's also a good idea to eliminate or adjust some of your habits that aren't serving you. For example, if you're in the habit of eating cookies or candy in the middle of the afternoon, you could replace this habit with eating carrot sticks instead. If you get rid of bad habits and replace them with better habits, you'll make it much easier for you to do what you need to do over the long term to be productive.

## Avoid Implementing Too Much Change Too Quickly

I t might sound enticing to make as much progress as you can on as many fronts as possible simultaneously. However, if you try to do too much too soon, it can backfire. You might find it to be too challenging to keep up your new routines for the long term, which could result in you dropping them altogether before they turn into a habit. When you start to implement a new habit for yourself, stick with that one habit until it's ingrained in your routine, then add more.

Think about what would likely happen if someone were to try to implement multiple habits at once. Let's say that the person in our example decides that they want to eat healthier food, exercise more, and get higher-quality rest. In the morning, the person would need to expend willpower fighting cravings for donuts and instead have a green drink for breakfast. The person would then need to expend additional willpower later in the day to go to the gym to work out. Finally, at night the person would need to use even more willpower to go to bed earlier than usual to meditate before bed and get more high-quality sleep.

These three new habits could significantly deplete the willpower of the person in our example. As a result, they might find it to be much more difficult to pay close attention at long meetings that are important but boring, and they might find it to be more challenging to tackle their most demanding projects at work. This could lead the person to focus on easier tasks that are less important while delaying important tasks that are more difficult to complete. Therefore, it's important to implement only one habit at a time until it's an established part of your routine. This increases your ability to continue performing the habit over the long term.

A benefit of implementing one habit at a time is that your success rate in implementing new habits will likely be much higher. Another advantage of this approach is that it reduces the likelihood you'll drain your willpower so much that you'll find yourself sleepwalking through the rest of your life.

## Practice Your New Routine Until it Becomes a Habit

T he amount of time it takes to implement a new habit can vary based on how much willpower it takes you to establish it and how much willpower it takes you to continue performing it.

For example, if you want to increase your level of fitness, you might find it to be relatively quick and easy to implement a habit of doing five push-ups each morning before you take a shower. Doing five push-ups does not take very much willpower, so it could take you only a few weeks before you start doing this automatically. However, if you instead want to implement a habit of doing 50 push-ups before you take a shower each morning, the increased willpower it takes to do 50 push-ups could result in this taking a few months to implement.

Consider rewarding yourself for performing your new habit and identify ways you can make the habit itself intrinsically rewarding. The more attractive you make it for you to perform the habit, the less time it will take you to establish it as an integral part of your routine.

## Be Specific Regarding What Each New Habit Entails

W hen you implement a new habit, the more detailed and specific you are regarding what the habit entails, the more likely it is that you'll do it. For example, if you start a new habit of doing five push-ups each morning, you could be more likely to follow through than if your new habit was more vague, such as a plan to work out each morning.

## People Close to You Might Resist Your Implementation of New Habits

A s you start to implement new habits, you might face resistance from people who are close to you. Thought leader Wyatt Woodsmall once remarked,

> *"People don't like it when you change, because the ways they use to manipulate you stop working."*

If the people around you genuinely care about you, they'll support positive changes you make in your life, including your implementation of new habits. However, don't let it stop you if you face some resistance from others as you change your life for the better. Sometimes you need to grow and move forward with your life to achieve bigger and better things even if others that should be there to support you actively resist you doing so.

The more success you achieve in your life, the more detractors and critics you'll have. People often criticize you as they see you becoming more successful because it makes it easier for them to live with the fact that you're moving forward with your life while they're standing still or moving backward in their own lives. If you face resistance from others as you start to implement new habits, consider it to be training in not paying attention to trolls. This will help you pay less attention to others who are critical of you in the future as you achieve even greater levels of success than what you're experiencing today.

# Chapter 6 – The Psychology and Neuroscience of Productivity

## How the Structure of Your Brain Influences Your Actions

W hen you have difficulty getting yourself to complete an important task, you're largely experiencing the more primitive parts of your brain fighting against your more evolved neocortex in a neurological war. For the sake of your productivity, you want the part of your brain called the neocortex to come out on top.

The human brain is very complex, but over the years, researchers have unraveled many of its mysteries. In this chapter, we're going to cover how you can supercharge your productivity by taking action on some of these insights.

One prominent researcher in the field of neuroscience was Dr. Paul MacLean, who developed the triune brain theory while he was part of the faculty at the Yale School of Medicine. This theory is a simplification of the complex and interconnected nature of the brain. However, it's a useful way to understand how the brain works. MacLean's triune brain theory describes how there are three distinct parts to the human brain that are built on top of one another.

The most primitive part of the brain, which is called the "lizard brain" or the "reptilian brain," is responsible for performing certain required functions to keep you alive. This includes basic activities, such as breathing, the maintenance of your heart rate and body temperature, and your fight or flight response. It also drives your desire to eat, drink, and enjoy other types of pleasure.

The next, more evolved part of your brain, is the limbic system, which is also known as the "mammalian brain" or the "emotional brain." This part of your brain is responsible for your feelings and emotions related to connecting with others.

The most evolved part of your brain is the neocortex, which is where your higher-order brain functions take place. This includes your use of critical thinking and your development and implementation of strategic plans. Your neocortex allows you to make logical and complex decisions, including abstract thinking.

At times, the most evolved part of your brain, the neocortex, might make it clear to you that it would be in your best interest to complete a certain task as soon as possible. However, you might simultaneously find yourself avoiding work on the task to get a snack, to chat with a colleague, or to spend time distracted by a shiny object. When this happens, you might be experiencing a conflict between the different parts of your brain.

It's human nature to want to minimize pain and maximize pleasure. However, focusing too much on near-term pleasure maximization can keep you from investing your time in endeavors that could offer you significant benefits over the long-term.

If the limbic and mammalian parts of your brain become too powerful, it could become increasingly difficult for you to avoid doing what's enjoyable in the near-term, even when this results in a significant reduction in your productivity. The better you become at keeping the impulses from the more primitive parts of your brain in check, the better you'll be able to achieve and sustain a high level of productivity over the long term. Therefore, the rest of this chapter contains actionable insights that can help you shift power away from the more primitive parts of your brain so you can supercharge the amount of activity that takes place in the most evolved part of your brain, the neocortex.

## Respect Your Future Self

It's easy to fall into the temptation of letting your "present self" avoid doing a difficult or tedious task by putting it off until later. However, this approach merely passes the task to your "future self" to complete at a later date.

If you don't feel like performing an undesirable task right now, it's unlikely you'll suddenly be excited about performing it at a later point in time. Also, if you're very busy right now, there's a good chance you'll also be busy in the future as new, unexpected tasks pop up. Therefore, respect your "future self" by tackling undesirable tasks as they come up rather than putting them off until later.

## Have an "Internal Locus of Control"

Y ou can be more productive if you have an "internal locus of control." This involves seeing yourself as being able to improve your capabilities rather than viewing your current skill set and abilities as fixed.

If you believe your skills and abilities are relatively fixed, you'll be less inclined to spend the time and effort required to enhance your capabilities. However, if you realize that you can improve, you'll be more likely to do what it takes to put in the work necessary to improve.

Especially if you manage people at work, it's important to see others as being capable of improving themselves. If someone on your team has consistently performed at a certain level, realize that with the right training, their performance can improve over time.

## Take Ownership

A nother psychological shift you can make to increase your productivity is to take full ownership of your areas of responsibility. This is the opposite of taking a "victim" mindset. By taking full ownership of your work, you'll increase your ability and willingness to overcome obstacles in your way, even if they were not your fault, to still achieve your objective.

Put yourself in the shoes of your boss or an important customer for your company. They don't want to hear a sob story about why you weren't able to complete a task. They have their own concerns and challenges, and they don't need you to add more to their plate. Instead, they want to receive the desired end product with the least amount of hassle possible. Even if others would put up with your excuses for not getting something done, it's important to set a higher bar for yourself.

If you encounter a challenge and you need to obtain your boss' buy-in before going forward, then do so. However, make sure you present your boss with a clear recommended solution along with alternative options rather than complaining that you have an unsolved problem.

Taking a step back, put yourself in the shoes of a customer. Imagine you almost forgot to order a birthday gift for someone close to you, and it's their birthday tomorrow. You ordered a gift and spent extra to have it shipped overnight so the package would arrive by tomorrow morning. Then let's say the package delivery company encounters blizzard conditions at the airport they were planning to use. If the delivery company can find an alternative solution and still get the package to the recipient of your gift on time, you'd likely be happy. However, if the package delivery company gives up and doesn't even try to re-route your package after seeing the blizzard, it's likely you wouldn't be as pleased. In this example, the package delivery company that went the extra mile to take ownership of the problem and delivered the gift on time was the more productive company. Be like that company.

There are plenty of examples in Hollywood movies where the main characters take full ownership for accomplishing their objectives. In my opinion, one of the best examples is Tom Cruise in the Mission Impossible series. If you haven't watched any of the Mission Impossible movies, I encourage you to watch at least one or two of them. While you watch, make mental or written notes on actionable insights you could apply in your own life. You'll experience a world-class level of ownership that could help you better see how you can react when seemingly impossible challenges arise.

Taking full ownership of your areas of responsibility can help you achieve a greater level of success. Think about this from the perspective of a boss or client that interacts with two very different people. One person regularly blames other people, technology, and nearly everything else for why their work contains significant mistakes and why their work doesn't get completed on time. In contrast, another person smoothly deals with problems as they come up, even if many of the challenges are unexpected or unfair, and still finds a way to get things done well and on time. It's hard to believe the "blaming" person would be viewed as favorably as the person who still manages to get things done, even when challenges arise.

## Change Your Interpretations for the Positive

As you go through your day, you can tell yourself a story about what's behind what you're experiencing. The story you tell yourself about the events you perceive in your life has an impact on your psychology, which itself can affect your level of productivity. Therefore, the more you can get yourself to generate positive interpretations of what you experience in your life, the more productive you can be.

When you interpret events positively, you keep your mind free of unproductive mental clutter. For example, imagine that your boss provides feedback on your recent work performance and says that ideally, you'd get the promotion you've been asking for in this promotion cycle. However, the funds to do so are not available in the budget right now. You could interpret this negatively or positively.

If you interpret your boss' statement negatively, you could take it to mean that your boss does not have the backbone to tell you that you're not likely to get promoted for the foreseeable future. Instead, your boss is merely using the excuse that your promotion is not in the company's budget right now as a convenient scapegoat excuse. Although this interpretation could be correct, it could lead to a reduction in your morale and your work quality. This, in turn, could make it harder for you and your boss to build a strong case for a promotion. Therefore, this pessimistic line of thinking could lead to you experiencing the specific negative outcome you were seeking to avoid.

If you interpret your boss' statement positively, you could take it to mean that your boss is supportive of you receiving a promotion. You could also interpret your boss' reference to the lack of funds in the current budget as a positive sign that when the funds become available, your boss will take the necessary steps to help you get promoted.

If you focus on the positive, you'll be more likely to feel you're moving toward accomplishing your objective of getting promoted. This can make it more likely that you'll continue to produce high-quality work. Even if your positive interpretation is not correct, if this mindset helps you continue to perform at a high level, it can increase the likelihood of you receiving a promotion when the funds are available in the budget.

## Manage Your Recurring Thoughts and Beliefs

In addition to monitoring how you interpret the events that take place in your life, it's also a good idea to assess your recurring thoughts and beliefs periodically to see if they're serving you. You can identify these beliefs by setting an alarm that will go off at specific times throughout the day. When the alarm goes off, write down what you were thinking about at that moment.

Based on the thoughts and beliefs you unearth, determine which ones are helpful or unhelpful to you, and then eliminate the unhelpful recurring thoughts from your mind. One way to get rid of unhelpful thoughts is to install positive thoughts and beliefs on top of them. For example, if you're new to programming in python and you're not very good at it yet, you might have a recurring thought that you don't know what you're doing, which is what some people call "imposter syndrome." You could replace this negative thought with a positive thought that you're developing a valuable skill set that will serve you later, and the challenges you're encountering and overcoming now are helping you build that expertise.

By applying these adjustments to your thought processes, you can help support your neocortex gain strength relative to the more primitive parts of your brain, which can help you increase your productivity.

# Chapter 7 – Customize Your Workspace for Enhanced Productivity

T here are more distractions today than at any other time in human history. However, you can adjust your workspace to overcome these distractions and create an environment that will foster consistently high levels of productivity.

There are three main steps to adjusting your workspace to increase your productivity. First, remove distractions. Second, tailor your workspace to better meet your needs. Third, organize your workspace. Also, if you work in an open office environment, there are additional adjustments you can make to further increase your productivity.

### Remove Distractions from Your Workspace

O ne of the easiest first steps to customize your workspace for enhanced productivity is to remove items that don't help you complete your work or that don't motivate you to keep making progress on your work. For example, if you have a stapler or paperclips on your desk but you only use them once a month, consider instead storing them in a drawer or somewhere else out of sight. However, if you have a picture of you and your family or friends and it puts a smile on your face, feel free to keep it on your desk even if it doesn't directly contribute to your work.

If you have something you're inclined to keep around for what it represents, but you don't want to keep the item itself, consider taking a picture of it and then tossing it. This way, you get to keep an image that represents the memory without having the physical item itself add clutter to your workspace.

## Organize Both the Physical and the Digital Areas of Your Workspace

Despite the significant shift toward a greater use of digital files, it's likely you still have a fair amount of hardcopy documents at your desk, such as slide decks and other handouts from recent meetings. If these paper files are not essential and you don't need to retain them, consider putting them in a bin to be shredded. This is not legal advice, but before you discard any documents, you might want to check to make sure they're not subject to a "hold" by the Legal Department at your company.

If you need to keep a document, consider scanning it into digitize it. By converting your hardcopy files to digital files, you can reduce the amount of paper clutter in your workspace. Also, you can use optical character recognition on the files you scan with software such as Adobe Acrobat to make your documents searchable. This can help you find information much more quickly when you need it.

### Increase Your Productivity in an Open Office Environment

Today most companies have an open office environment with open concept floor plans. In this type of working environment, there are relatively few partitions between desks, and any partitions between desks are relatively short. This represents a significant shift from a formerly popular office environment that consisted of cubicles with relatively high partitions between desks. There are several advantages to employers when they shift to an open office environment, including cost savings, more natural light, and increased collaboration among employees. However, there are also several disadvantages associated with open office environments, including a lack of privacy, increased noise, more distractions, and employees experiencing more frequent interruptions from their coworkers.

The extent to which an open office environment can increase or decrease the productivity of specific employees at a company is partly based on the type of work the employees perform. For example, an open office environment could be more beneficial for employees who perform work that requires significant on-going collaboration, such as consultants, marketers, and project managers. However, an open office environment might not increase employees' productivity if they perform work that typically requires relatively little collaboration.

If you find yourself working in an open office environment, there are still some things you can do to increase your productivity. You can use headphones to drown out distracting noises and reduce the likelihood others will stop by your desk and interrupt your work. Depending on your company culture, you could ask your manager about working remotely at least once or twice a week.

If you're working on something that requires a high level of concentration, consider reserving a meeting room to complete that task. If your company has a cafeteria, training center, or conference center, those areas often have places where you can get focused work done in peace during off-hours.

## Tips for Being Productive When You Work Remotely

W orking remotely can help you to be more productive. For example, one of the most significant advantages of working remotely is that you'll likely be subject to fewer distractions, such as coworkers stopping by your desk, which can interrupt your work. Also, the elimination of your commute to and from work on the days you work remotely can also contribute to a higher level of productivity. However, there are common pitfalls to avoid when you work remotely.

When you work from home, it's not uncommon for people in your personal life to reach out to you as if you aren't working. For example, if you have a spouse or a roommate, they might interrupt you thinking that because you're not at the office, you're not working. To keep this from being an issue, establish clear boundaries, and let those people know that although you're at home, it's your responsibility to get your work done. Designate a space in your home where you can do your work, and make it clear to others when they can and can't come and talk to you. For example, you can put a whiteboard on the door to your home office with a message that indicates when you can't be interrupted. You could also coordinate with others in your home that if they see you wearing a specific article of clothing, such as a baseball cap, this is a signal that you're working and that it's not a good time for them to interrupt you.

If you work remotely from a coffee shop or other social setting, you could be subject to significant background noise and distractions. If this is the case, keep headphones or earplugs in the bag you use to carry your laptop, which can help prevent these sounds from distracting you. If you're sitting in a public place, consider facing a wall instead of facing an area where there's a significant amount of activity. Although a wall does not provide you with the same type of people watching another view could, facing a wall can reduce the number of distractions you experience. However, if the work you're performing on your laptop is confidential, keep your screen from being viewed by others even if it results in you experiencing more visual distractions.

In some remote working environments, you might have an Internet connection that's not reliable. To reduce the extent to which this could reduce your productivity, consider signing up for an unlimited data plan for your smartphone that lets you use it as a hotspot. This provides you with a backup option in case you find yourself in an area where you cannot connect with Wi-Fi.

## Consciously Eliminate Distractions

M odern technology has made our lives much easier in many ways, but it has brought with it a wide array of new technological intrusions, such as smartphone notifications, that add to the existing variety of workplace distractions. For example, while you're trying to get your work done, on any given day, you might find yourself interrupted by a constant barrage of emails, phone calls, and last-minute meetings. This doesn't even include urgent requests for you to provide help, offer feedback, or otherwise assist others right away. These abundant distractions can cause you to experience a massive reduction in your productivity without you even realizing it. Therefore, it's important to identify and reduce the impact of as many of these distractions as possible.

One way to reduce visual distractions is to consider what's in your peripheral view as you work. For example, if the view from your workspace is not likely to be distracting, such as when you face trees or a wall, this could help your productivity. However, it can be distracting if you can see significant activity while you work, even if it's only in your peripheral vision. This could include a busy street, coworkers standing around and talking, or airplanes flying by. You won't always be able to remove all the visual distractions where you work, but it's a good idea to do what you can to minimize the impact of distracting surroundings. Don't let yourself be at the mercy of these distractions by letting them pull you away from your most important work. Instead, consciously identify your most significant distractions and take action to reduce or eliminate them where you can.

Also, consider adjusting the way you use your phone to keep it from distracting you. This might include putting your phone in airplane mode while you work, disabling notifications temporarily with "do not disturb" functionality, or by simply turning your phone off. You can also reduce the likelihood that you'll let your phone distract you by putting it out of sight in a place that is relatively difficult to reach, such as in a locked drawer.

### Overcome Auditory Distractions

A uditory distractions can be even more distracting than visual distractions. When your work environment is too noisy, it can be challenging to concentrate. Therefore, it's crucial that you also address any auditory distractions you might experience in your workspace.

One of the best ways to drown out distracting noise as you

work is to put on headphones and listen to music. However, certain types of music tend to help you to be more productive than others, and there's also a personal element when it comes to music. Music that helps someone else be more productive might not be the best type of music to help you be more productive. Therefore, it's a good idea to experiment with different types of music to see what works best for you.

Even if it doesn't seem like it at the time, listening to music with lyrics might distract you, especially if you start silently singing along in your head. Therefore, consider listening to instrumental music without lyrics. Although classical music and electronic music are some of the most popular forms of instrumental music, there are other great options available to you. For example, you can listen to nature music that replicates jungle sounds, waves crashing, or a thunderstorm. You can also listen to instrumental video game music, which is designed to keep the listener alert and engaged. That can be the perfect type of music if you want to stay motivated to continue working on a project. My personal favorite is listening to thunderstorms. I find it relaxing, and it also drowns out a wide variety of noise, which leads us to the next point.

It can be helpful to choose music that covers up the type of sound around you. If you're working in a relatively noisy environment, you might want to listen to "noisier" music. For example, if you listen to classical music in a noisy environment, you might hear a significant amount of noise around you even while you're listening to music. However, if you instead listen to music with more "noise" in it, such as thunderstorms, you might barely notice the background noise in the environment around you.

It can also be helpful to listen to music that is lower energy. Music that is too high energy can make it difficult for you to sit still and perform high-quality work for more than a short amount of time. However, if you find yourself in a rut, listening to higher-energy music for a short amount of time can help you get out of it.

You can also listen to a single song on repeat to associate it with a specific task. For example, you might listen to one song while you batch process a variety of lower-value tasks, such as organizing files. This way, your mind can more clearly differentiate when it needs to be thinking deeply and focusing versus when it can take a bit of a break as you work on less thought intensive tasks.

Consider using playlists of specific music tailored to different types of tasks. As you come across songs that you think will help you to be more productive as you listen to them, you can add them to a custom playlist so you can listen to only the very best songs to keep you in the zone as you complete your work.

## Match the Type of Headphones You Use to Your Work Environment

E specially if you work in a noisy environment, using headphones consistently can be one of the simplest, easiest, and most effective changes you can make to significantly increase your productivity. Given the importance of using headphones, we're going to cover the benefits and disadvantages of using different types of headphones.

Over-the-ear headphones can do a better job of blocking outside noise, but a disadvantage of this type of headphones is that they're generally too large to fit into your pocket. Therefore, the large size of these headphones might keep you from carrying them around as much. For example, if you unexpectedly find yourself waiting in a long line at lunch with a guy talking loudly on his cell phone behind you, you could pull out smaller headphones from your pocket and listen to a podcast, audiobook, or music. However, if you only use larger over-the-ear headphones that don't fit in a pocket, you might find yourself wanting to use headphones without them being available to you.

One advantage of using over-the-ear headphones is that if you combine them with smaller in-ear earbud headphones, you'll have an especially strong ability to drown out a noisy working environment. You can do this by first putting in the smaller in-ear earbud headphones and then putting on the larger over-the-ear headphones. You could then use a headphone splitter to have the sound go to both of the headphones you're wearing. An alternative is to first put in earplugs and then put on your over-the-ear headphones, which also does an outstanding job of blocking especially loud outside noise.

In-ear earbud headphones can provide you with high-quality sound in a small package that's easy to carry around with you. I use this type of headphones almost exclusively, and I appreciate the convenience of the small size that you can easily carry anywhere.

Although they're typically more expensive, you can also consider obtaining noise-canceling headphones. Noise-canceling headphones are now sold both as over-the-ear headphones and as in-ear earbud headphones.

## Tailor Your Workspace to Better Meet Your Needs

At least once a year, take a step back and see if there are any opportunities to better customize your workspace, so it better meets your needs. For example, you might find that it would help you to get a whiteboard to make your most important tasks more visible to you. Alternatively, if your work environment has become noisier, you might benefit from getting yourself some headphones or earplugs to work more effectively without distraction. Also, you might notice that you don't have anything personalizing your workspace, and adding some pictures to your desk could make you feel more at home. It's not as important what specific customizations you make. Instead, it's more important to adjust your workspace closer to an environment that would help you feel more engaged and focused, which can help you achieve a higher level of productivity.

You can add items to your workspace that remind you of your

most important goals. However, if any of your goals are some-what private, you might not want to display them written out explicitly where your coworkers could see them. Therefore, ra-ther than displaying the actual words that represent your goals, consider using symbols to represent them. For example, if one of your goals is to get promoted, you can have a picture on your desk of someone climbing Mount Everest. Only you will know that this picture represents your goal to get promoted. When your coworkers see this picture, they could interpret it as an indica-tion that you like hiking in the mountains without realizing the deeper hidden meaning.

Also, consider including a few meaningful items in your work-space that serve as clear reminders of who you are, what you want to accomplish, and why you want to achieve what you're going after. Here are some examples. You could keep a small statue of the "hear no evil, see no evil, and speak no evil monkeys" at your desk, which could help you remind yourself that blocking out unnecessary distractions can help you improve your productiv-ity. You could keep an empty frame on your desk where you plan to later include a picture of yourself holding an award for a spe-cific accomplishment. Whichever items you choose, make sure they're personally meaningful to you.

It can also help your productivity to adjust the temperature of the room where you work or the clothing you wear so you can be at the ideal temperature for you to perform your best work. A temperature around 70 degrees Fahrenheit, or approximately 21 degrees Celsius, generally fosters productivity more than much hotter or much colder temperatures. Depending on where you work, you might not be able to adjust the thermostat. However, you can address this by wearing multiple layers of clothing and adjusting what you wear as necessary.

Consider adjusting the lighting in your workspace. If your office environment is too dark, it can cause eye strain and po-tentially a reduction in your productivity. You might be able to bring in an additional lamp or desk light to help add more light to your workspace. However, if you're not able to bring extra lighting, see if you can adjust the blinds near where you sit to change the amount of sunlight that enters the room.

If you spend a significant amount of your working time using a computer, consider using multiple monitors in your workspace. Using more than one monitor is especially useful when you need to work with multiple files at the same time. If you're able to use multiple monitors, consider flipping one of your monitors 90 degrees from landscape to portrait, which will allow you to view larger sections of documents more easily. If you have the freedom to choose your own computer monitor, such as what you use for your home office, consider using a 4K television instead of traditional computer monitors.

Your ability to use multiple monitors is not limited to elaborate office setups. Even if you travel frequently and need to work while you're on the go, you can still benefit from using multiple monitors. For example, you could use a dual-screen laptop, such as the Asus ZenBook Pro Duo. This laptop's main screen has a 4k resolution, and its secondary screen is approximately half the size of the main screen. Even if you don't buy a laptop that has two screens, you can purchase additional screens that you can attach to your existing laptop, which can help you improve your productivity while you're working on the road.

It's also a good idea to always have at least one way that is quick and easy for you to make a note of ideas that come to you. For example, you could write your ideas down on sticky notes, a whiteboard, a spreadsheet, or an app on your smartphone, such as Evernote or OneNote. Regardless of which format you use to take down your ideas, make sure you review these ideas periodically so you can remember to take action on the ones that make sense for you to pursue.

In addition to customizing your primary workspace to better meet your needs, there are also benefits to occasionally working in a different environment. For example, if you need to work on something that requires significant creativity or focused thought, consider working briefly in a new workspace, such as a park, a nearby university library, or a coffee shop.

## Organize Your Workspace

I f your workspace is a chaotic and disorganized mess, it can cause you unnecessary frustration in addition to reducing your productivity. Also, when your boss or an important client reaches out to you and needs something right away, it's import-ant that you can easily find what you need rather than having to rummage around looking for it. Therefore, it's generally worth it to organize your workspace.

In addition to organizing your physical workspace, it's at least as important to organize your digital workspace. This includes your digital files as well as shortcuts to important folders, appli-cations, and web pages. Remove junk that clutters your ability to find files you might need to access. If you have many files and shortcuts on the desktop of your computer, either delete them or move them to a long-term storage folder that's out of your way. This will keep you from wasting time searching around through junk files and links to find the files and shortcuts you need.

In addition to removing unused shortcuts, you can save your-self time by adding easily accessible shortcuts to your most fre-quently accessed files, folders, and programs. This will help you spend less of your time looking for things, which frees up more time for you to get your work done.

Spend at least a few minutes organizing your workspace at the end of your workday. This includes clearing away any disor-ganized documents or other items, but it doesn't stop there. It's also a good idea to set out any documents or other things you'll need to start leveraging when you return to work the next day. For example, if you have some handwritten notes for a presenta-tion you're going to present the next afternoon, place these notes in a location in your workspace where they would be very easily accessible to you. This keeps you from having to look around for these notes the next day, which helps you hit the ground running when you return to work. However, especially if your company has a "clean desk" policy, it's important to avoid leaving any sensitive documents on your desk where anyone walking by could access them.

## Digitize Your Paper Files

I t's not uncommon to have multiple stacks of unorganized papers on your desk, in your desk drawers, or elsewhere. If you don't take action to address this, as time passes, you could find yourself in possession of even larger stacks of paper as you receive printed presentations, memos, and other reference materials at meetings. Having many large stacks of paper can make it somewhat challenging to find specific documents you need due to the sheer volume. You might not be able to discard some especially important documents, even if you digitize them. However, by digitizing as many files as you can, over time, you can likely get rid of the vast majority of the paper files in your workspace.

When you digitize documents, the obvious part of the process is to scan in the paper files to convert them into a digital format, such as PDF or JPG. You can use digital scanners designed specifically for this purpose, or you could use a smartphone app, such as Adobe Scan, to perform your scanning. Before you digitize your documents, make sure that this wouldn't violate any policies or security protocols your company has for highly sensitive documents.

After you scan in your paper files, you can then process them with optical character recognition, which is also known as OCR. You can use programs such as Adobe Acrobat to OCR your files, which enables you to search them. This can make it much easier for you to locate specific keywords in your digitized documents.

After you're done digitizing your paper documents, you can store the digitized versions of your files in a location on your computer or in the cloud where you can easily access them in the future. If some of the documents you digitize are of exception-ally high importance, consider saving them in multiple different locations, such as your computer's hard drive, your team's shared drive, and separately in the cloud. This can help you increase your likelihood of maintaining access to these important documents even if your hard drive unexpectedly crashes. Although it can take some time to digitize your paper documents, when you need to access them in the future, you'll be glad you did.

# Chapter 8 – Lists Can Help You Increase Your Productivity

Y ou can take greater control over your workload by using the right types of lists in the right way, which can help you accomplish your most important objectives more quickly and with less effort. However, many people have not had great experiences using the traditional to-do list.

A drawback of the traditional to-do list is that it only lists out the things you need to do without providing clear guidance on which tasks you should prioritize. Also, when to-do lists contain too many tasks, this type of list can contribute to overwhelm and anxiety that there are some items on the list that you might not ever get around to finishing.

In this chapter, we're going to go over more effective ways of using lists. We'll cover several different types of lists, but you don't have to use them all. Instead, experiment with them and then use only those lists that you find to be the most useful for you.

## Types of Lists

T he two most important lists are an Everything To-Do List and a Daily To-Do List, which I highly recommend that you consider implementing. An Everything To-Do List is a relatively long list of things you either have to do or that you might want to do. A Daily To-Do List is a list of the tasks you intend to complete within the next 24 hours. Each day, you can use your Everything To-Do List as a reference for tasks you might want to include in your next Daily To-Do List.

The following examples of lists are less critical than an Everything To-Do List and a Daily To-Do List, but they can also help you increase your productivity. However, this is only a starting point, and there's no limit to the number of lists you can create.

A Greatest Accomplishments and Failures List helps you identify your most significant historical successes and setbacks. You can look over your greatest historical accomplishments to make it crystal clear to you how capable you are of overcoming significant obstacles to achieve great things. Keeping tabs on your greatest failures helps you learn from your past mistakes and realize that even significant failures can't keep you down for long.

A Key Concerns List is the list you use to write down any concerns that are on your mind, which could include things you need to follow up on or that you need to remember to do. This can help you reduce your mental clutter and free up your ability to achieve a greater level of focus. Also, having a clear list of your key concerns can help you take more control over them, which can increase your ability to be more proactive in addressing them.

A Don't Do List contains things that are not a good use of your time and that you want to stop doing. This list can help you free up time and energy that you can instead devote to pursuing higher-value activities.

A Rejuvenation List contains the things that are most effective at restoring your energy and your ability to focus. You can use this list when your level of energy or focus is low or when something requires you to be at your peak performance. Three examples of categories that can contribute significantly to rejuvenation are exercise, nutrition, and rest, although everyone is different.

A Commitment List is a list of the things you've committed to providing to others and the things you're waiting on from other people. This list can help you stay on top of your obligations, and it can make it easier for you to identify items where you need to follow up on something. For each item you add to this list, make a clear note regarding what the deliverable is, the name and contact information of the other party to the commitment, and the date by which each deliverable needs to be submitted.

A Bucket List includes things that you want to do or experience in your lifetime. This could include places around the world you want to visit or experiences you want to have, such as skydiving or scuba diving.

## Electronic Lists Versus Paper Lists

T he format in which you maintain your lists is a matter of personal preference. Feel free to experiment with both electronic and paper lists to see what works best for you. Also, you don't need to use the same type of list format exclusively. For example, you could keep all your lists in an electronic format while also writing out your Daily To-Do List on a sticky note or whiteboard so you can make the tasks on this list more visible to you.

One of the main benefits of using paper lists is that they can be more visible to you. For example, if you have your Daily To-Do List written down on a piece of paper at your desk, you can easily reference the tasks on this list simply by glancing over at it. In contrast, to see the tasks in an electronic list, you would need to spend additional time and effort to locate and open the electronic file that contains your lists.

Although electronic lists are not for everyone, there are many benefits to using a spreadsheet tool such as Excel, Google Sheets, or Calc rather than paper lists. One of the most obvious benefits is that spreadsheets are quicker and easier to edit compared to paper lists. Also, if you maintain your lists in a spreadsheet, you can filter and sort the items on your lists based on multiple criteria, such as priority, due date, or estimated time to complete.

If you prefer, you could instead maintain your lists using a word processing application, such as Word, or a note-taking application, such as Evernote or OneNote. However, regardless of which electronic format you choose, a benefit is that if you save these lists in the cloud, you can edit them from anywhere on your smartphone, tablet, or laptop. Also, if you want some of your electronic lists to be more visible and accessible to you throughout the day, you can print them out so you can have them more readily available to you.

## Best Practices for Working with Tasks on Your Lists

If you have many tasks competing for your attention, it can be difficult to determine which ones would be the best use of your time. You can overcome this challenge by making a note of the due date for each task, if applicable, as well as each task's importance, such as low, medium, or high. By including these two data points for each task in your list, you can make a more informed decision about which tasks would represent the best use of your time.

Consider using a moderately aggressive due date for each of your tasks. It's a good idea to set a personal deadline that's much more aggressive than the completion date you share with others. This way, if you find that you need to do more work on a task by the time your personal deadline arrives, you won't fail to meet a due date you promised someone else. However, if you don't meet one of your personal deadlines, find out why you missed it, and apply those lessons learned going forward to keep it from happening again. This will help you maintain a cushion between your internal and external due dates.

It can be tempting to fill your Daily To-Do List with tasks that are easy because of the satisfaction that comes with checking items off your list. However, it's important to avoid this temptation by instead including only those tasks that are the most critical for you to complete within the next 24 hours. If you choose a set of tasks that is approximately the right level of difficulty for you, you'll be more likely to enter into what Mihaly Csikszentmihalyi calls a "flow state" at the edge of your comfort zone, where you're especially productive.

If you regularly give yourself an excessive workload on your Daily To-Do List, you could be more likely to lose the motivation to continue performing at a high level. An overloaded Daily To-Do List can also make it more difficult for you to handle new things that come up unexpectedly. When things come up that are a higher priority than anything you were targeting to do on a particular day, re-prioritize your Daily To-Do List so you can remain focused on completing your highest value tasks.

It can be helpful to identify which of your tasks you can easily perform in a batch with other related tasks. For example, if you need to call a few people, it would likely be more efficient for you to perform all these calls back to back. Otherwise, if you instead call these people at various times throughout the day, you'll need to mentally shift in and out of your thought process for making these calls. By batch processing these tasks together, you can avoid the task-switching costs associated with going back and forth between this type of task and other types of tasks throughout the day.

If you frequently find yourself in vastly different work environments, it can be useful to specify in your Daily To-Do List where you could most efficiently perform each task. For example, if a task requires you to work with multiple files at the same time, you might be more productive in an environment where you have access to multiple computer monitors. In contrast, if you're working on a relatively simple task that involves using only one file, you might be able to easily complete this task on your laptop in any environment. By specifying where you can most efficiently complete your tasks, you'll be better able to identify which tasks are the best use of your time based on your current work environment.

Consider adding a pre-specified reward for completing each of your tasks. This will help motivate you to complete your tasks because you'll see an enjoyable short-term reward associated with getting to the finish line. This could be as simple as going for a brief walk or taking a snack or coffee break.

## Checklists

C hecklists are a special type of list where you follow a pre-specified series of steps to increase the accuracy, speed, and consistency of your work. Checklists can decrease the likelihood that you'll miss a critical step in a process. For example, even pilots with a few decades of experience go through a pre-flight checklist to ensure they don't forget to perform important steps.

One of the most valuable uses of a checklist is to make it extremely easy for someone to quickly and accurately perform a task with little to no guidance, even if they've never completed the task before.

Checklists can also be one of the most effective tools for developing a smoothly functioning delegation system. When you use a checklist to delegate work, you'll be able to spend less time explaining how to complete a task, you'll receive far fewer questions, and it's also more likely that the final work product will contain relatively few errors.

There are two types of checklists. The first is a Read-Do checklist, which is a relatively detailed step-by-step guide on how to perform a specific task. The person using this type of checklist reads the first step before they do the first step, after which they repeat this process for the remaining steps until the task is complete. For example, few people have ever used a heart defibrillator before. Therefore, defibrillators located in office environments typically include an easy-to-follow Read-Do checklist that explains how to use it. This checklist is designed in such a way that even someone doing the task for the first time could follow the steps and use the machine properly. For Read-Do checklists, make sure you provide sufficient details to make it abundantly clear what the person using the checklist needs to do.

Clarity is especially important for Read-Do checklists because people who are unfamiliar with how to perform a task might need substantial guidance on how to perform all the steps in the process, especially if it's their first time doing it. For Read-Do checklists, consider including a brief description of common mistakes people make along with guidance on how to avoid them.

The second type of checklist is a Do-Confirm checklist, which generally includes only a list of things that need to be done without any details on how to accomplish those steps. The purpose of this type of checklist is to ensure the person using it doesn't forget to perform a step. An example is a checklist of things a pilot needs to do before takeoff. This checklist might include an inspection of the outside of the plane. However, it excludes granular details regarding everything the pilot should look for during this inspection of the plane.

Although clarity is still important for Do-Confirm checklists, brevity is more important. This is because the purpose of this checklist is to ensure that someone who performs a task frequently doesn't skip any steps, and this type of person typically already knows how to perform each step. Where possible, keep the size of Do-Confirm checklists to no more than one page, and ideally no more than half a page.

If you implement checklists and you find them to be useful, consider revisiting their content at least once a year. By reassessing your checklists annually, you can keep them up to date and refine them as necessary to ensure they continue to remain effective and useful for you and your team. During your annual assessment of your checklists, you can also determine if it would make sense to create additional checklists for some of your team's other processes.

# Chapter 9 – Identify and Implement Process Improvements

W ould you want to use the same smartphone for a decade? Probably not. With the improvements in technology that will likely take place, a smartphone released ten years from now might be unimaginably more useful to you than today's latest devices. Similarly, don't settle for continuing to use the same processes to perform your work without periodically checking to make sure they're the best way for you to do things.

The Japanese concept of kaizen, which means continuous improvement, is an excellent mindset for you to have when you think about the processes you use to complete your work. Although improving your work processes has a high level of importance, it usually has a low level of urgency. However, if you proactively take action to improve your processes, you can be much more productive while simultaneously making it much easier for you to complete your work.

Even if a process was efficient and effective at one point in the past, as circumstances change at your company and as new technologies become available in your industry, the old way of doing things could become obsolete. Although process improvements can have a significant impact on your productivity, you don't have to completely reinvent what you do. If you implement small process improvements consistently, over time, you'll find that you can complete the same amount of work you're producing today significantly faster and with more accuracy.

We're going to go over three ways you can improve your processes. First, we'll cover how you can identify and eliminate unnecessary work. This could include pinpointing unnecessary steps in a process or even an entire process that you could discontinue. Second, we're going to go over how you can redesign your processes to make them more efficient and effective. Third, we'll go over how you can automate your processes so you can get your work done faster, more accurately, and with less effort.

## Eliminate Unnecessary Work

One way to be more productive is to identify tasks you perform that could be reduced or eliminated. It's a good idea to perform this assessment before you start thinking about how you can redesign or automate your processes to avoid spending your time adjusting processes that don't need to be performed in the first place. When you begin identifying if there's any work you can eliminate, start with the tasks that take the greatest amount of time and effort to complete. This can help you more efficiently identify significant amounts of work you can discontinue performing.

If you come across a task or a part of a task that you think you could eliminate, but you're not quite sure, think about what the negative consequences would be, if any, if you simply stopped performing the task. Also, consider whether the task is being performed too close to perfection when perfection isn't needed. This can help you cut back at least part of the work for a task that is not necessary.

As you think more deeply about a task, you might realize that it would make more sense for someone else to perform the work. This could involve you delegating the work to someone else on your team, or it could involve shifting the work from your team to another team at your company, which could eliminate your personal need to perform the work.

## Redesign Your Processes to Make Them More Efficient and Effective

Process improvements can include developing a more efficient way to complete work, increasing the quality of the output produced by the process, or changing how frequently you perform the process.

One easy way to make your processes more efficient is to make at least one small incremental improvement each time you perform it. For example, if you use a spreadsheet to complete a monthly task, make at least one incremental improvement to the spreadsheet every time you use it, which could involve automating some of the work. Over time these small adjustments can result in a much more efficient process.

An excellent starting point for increasing the quality of the output of one of your processes is to talk to the end consumer of the related deliverable. The more you deeply understand what the customer of your process wants, the better you'll be able to increase the quality of your output. For example, let's say you submit a 10-page memo to your team's Vice President once a month that summarizes key developments related to your work. By reaching out to the consumer of this memo, you can better understand what adjustments could be made to increase its quality. This could involve shortening the memo, including more graphs and charts, or adjusting the format to a PowerPoint slide deck.

Another way to improve your team's processes is to revisit how frequently you perform each task. This can help you identify areas where you can reduce your workload while simultaneously getting the same or better results. For example, your team might need to take time each year to negotiate an updated annual contract with a third-party vendor. However, if you're confident your team will need this service for the foreseeable future, you could adjust the contract renewal cycle to once every two or three years instead of an annual renewal. Alternatively, you could shift to using an evergreen contract. In addition to saving your team the time and effort required to renew the contract each year, you might also be able to save your company money with a long-term contract discount. However, before you agree to a multi-year contract, make sure you trust the vendor to deliver quality services, and be sure you'll continue to need those services at least for the duration of the contract.

## Automate Your Processes

I f your team performs repetitive tasks regularly, consider automating them. Automating a task typically requires an upfront expenditure of time and effort. However, automation can save you a significant amount of time, and it can also increase the accuracy of the task being performed due to fewer manual errors taking place.

# Chapter 10 – Put Time on Your Side

## Work in Blocks of Uninterrupted Time

Y ou can increase your productivity by working in blocks of uninterrupted time, such as 60 or 90 minutes at a time. These blocks of time should be long enough for you to build momentum and achieve a significant amount of progress. However, these blocks of time should not be so long that you would burn yourself out, which could reduce your productivity.

By working in blocks of uninterrupted time, you'll also increase your ability to get in the zone. In his book "Flow," Mihaly Csikszentmihalyi covers what it means to be in the zone, which the author calls flow. One of the most important ways you can structure your work to put yourself into a flow state is to do work that is at just the right level of difficulty for you so that it's not too easy and not too hard. Then, once you're working in a flow state, your momentum makes you want to keep going.

## Use Buffer Blocks of Time

I f your calendar is full of meetings, you might find it to be challenging to find time to get your work done. If you want to take back control over your time, you can add buffer blocks of time to your calendar. During these buffer blocks of time, you can focus on getting your own most important work done. Given that your work calendar will be blocked off at these times, other people at your company are less likely to add you to a meeting during these times. This can reduce the number of meetings you need to attend, which can help you free up time to get your own work done.

If an administrative assistant manages your calendar, let them know that these buffer blocks of time deserve the same level of respect as your other meetings. In other words, if someone asks if you're free during one of your buffer blocks, the answer would be a definite "no."

While you're working in one of your uninterrupted blocks of time, unexpected emergencies might require you to stop your work to address them. If an interruption you experience is a legitimate emergency, realize that this is a fact of life, and don't worry about stepping away momentarily from your work. However, if the item is not truly an emergency, consider taking a step back to see if there are any actions you could take that would keep this from happening again as frequently in the future.

In addition to using buffer blocks of time to get your work done, you can also use them occasionally to smooth out the logistics for other meetings or events in your personal life. For example, if you have a doctor's appointment at noon, block off your calendar for some additional time before and after the appointment to give yourself time to get there and back. This reduces the likelihood someone would include you in a meeting during this time.

## Put Your Most Important Tasks on Your Calendar

When you identify the key tasks you plan to accomplish during a specific day, you can block off time on your calendar to complete these tasks to increase the likelihood you'll finish them. This is one way you can use the buffer blocks of time mentioned above.

When you start using buffer blocks of time to complete your most important tasks, use them sparingly. If you fill up a large portion of your calendar with buffer blocks, you might not take them very seriously. Also, if you block off too much of your calendar, your schedule might not be sufficiently flexible to allow you to tackle things that arise unexpectedly. The fewer the number of buffer blocks you schedule on your calendar, the more they'll stand out, and the more seriously you'll take them.

When you're deciding if it makes sense to add one of your

most important tasks to your calendar in a buffer block, consider whether the task is time-sensitive. Also, consider if you've found it to be difficult for you to get yourself to make significant progress on the task either due to other priorities or your own procrastination. If either of these situations applies, you should seriously consider adding the task to your calendar as part of a buffer block of time.

## Take Advantage of Your Most Productive Times of the Day

Y ou can increase your productivity by identifying the time of day when you tend to have more energy and are more focused. Although everyone has peaks and troughs in their level of energy, many people find that they have the highest level of energy in the first few hours of their workday. If this is the case for you, it's not a bad idea to start your day by working on your most challenging task so you can get it out of the way and build momentum for the rest of your day. Otherwise, this task could figuratively hang over your head until you finish it, which could result in you being less productive. However, if you're not a morning person and you tend to have a relatively low level of energy when you start your workday, it could make more sense for you to save your hardest tasks for the time of day when you tend to be the most energized.

If you notice your current level of energy and your ability to focus are inadequate for you to work effectively on your highest priority task, there are two options available to you. First, you can do something that would increase your level of energy and your ability to focus. This could be the perfect time for you to do something on your Rejuvenation List, which is a list of the things you've found to be most effective at restoring your energy and your ability to focus. Your second option would be to instead work on a task with a lower priority that you still have the energy and focused attention to perform. By noticing when your level of energy and ability to focus is not sufficient to complete a task effectively, you can avoid spinning your wheels and make more progress for each minute you work.

At this point, you might have only a vague idea of the time of day when you typically have the highest level of energy and are best able to tackle your most challenging tasks. Therefore, we're going to go over two ways you can identify the time of day when you tend to have the most or the least amount of energy.

First, you can use hourly check-ins with yourself regarding your energy level. For a few days in a row, you can set an alert once an hour that will ask you to rate your current level of energy on a scale from one to five, with five indicating that you feel the most energetic.

Second, you can take a central nervous system (CNS) tap test once an hour for a few days in a row. This test measures the current status of your central nervous system, and it can provide a proxy for your level of energy. The test, which you can perform with an app on your smartphone or tablet, involves you tapping your screen as rapidly as you can for a short amount of time, such as ten seconds. For this exercise, a more rapid rate of tapping would be indicative of a higher level of energy. An alternative to using a CNS tap test app on your smartphone or tablet is to set a timer for ten seconds and manually count how many taps you're able to complete before the time runs out.

You can then type the results from the two tests above into a spreadsheet so you can identify patterns. Ideally, you want to maintain substantially the same routine during these days, such as going to bed and waking up at approximately the same time each day. If this doesn't produce clear patterns, it's possible that collecting additional data over a few more days could help.

## Batch Processing

I f you need to perform the same type of task many times, you can usually increase your productivity by batch processing these tasks all at once rather than completing them separately at different times throughout your workday. Batch processing is especially useful for your lower-priority tasks that are less time-sensitive. It can also be helpful to use this strategy if you need to prepare in a specific way for similar meetings. For example, if you manage others and have check-in meetings with them weekly, consider scheduling all of these meetings on the same day back to back. This type of strategy helps you avoid task-switching costs, which include the time and effort it takes you to mentally switch from working on one kind of task to working on a completely different task.

Although batch processing can be useful, for tasks you could easily address within a few minutes, it's typically a good idea to get them done right away rather than saving them and processing them later as part of a larger batch.

When you're batch processing tasks that don't require much concentration, consider multitasking. This can include listening to audiobooks, podcasts, or even learning a new language while you complete your less thought-intensive tasks.

## Multitasking and Single-Tasking

Multitasking can be useful for routine tasks that require little thought. For example, it's likely that you can simultaneously work out at the gym and listen to music without any significant issues. However, for non-routine tasks that require considerable thought and attention, it's generally a better idea to focus on one task at a time.

Behavioral Science Professor Nick Chater found that humans can do two things at once if the tasks are routine and well-practiced. However, if you try to perform multiple tasks at the same time that are non-routine and complicated, it's not possible to multitask in the true sense of the word. Instead, if you try to perform multiple non-routine and complicated tasks at the same time, you're merely rapidly switching between these tasks. This results in significant task-switching costs, which can reduce your productivity.

Especially for people who multitask regularly, it can take some effort to switch to performing more single-tasking. One way to improve your ability to focus on one thing at a time is to meditate. Meditation can be as simple as focusing on nothing but your breath for a few minutes. Another way to improve your ability to focus is to gradually increase the amount of time you spend in one sitting focused on performing a single task.

## Taking Breaks

A lthough it might be counterintuitive, you can accomplish more by taking regular breaks. To clarify, this isn't referring to you accomplishing more for each minute that you work. Instead, this refers to an increased total level of output. In other words, if you work continuously for four hours, you'll likely accomplish less than if you instead work for 55 minutes at a time while taking a 5-minute break each hour.

If you're incredibly motivated to accomplish something, you might be reluctant to do anything but work nonstop until you complete it. You might think that you're being too easy on yourself if you take short breaks throughout the day. However, even some of the most driven people in history realized that they would accomplish more by taking breaks.

For example, John D. Rockefeller realized that he could be more productive by taking breaks. In his biography of Rockefeller titled "Tycoon," author Ron Chernow stated that Rockefeller was in the habit of

> *"napping daily after lunch...Rockefeller didn't do this in a purely recreational spirit but mingled work and rest to pace himself and improve his productivity."*

Chernow noted that although Rockefeller was fond of taking an afternoon nap, he

> *"never wasted time on frivolities. Even his daily breaks – the*

*midmorning snack of crackers and milk and the postprandial nap – were designed to conserve energy and help him to strike an ideal balance between his physical and mental forces."*

The pioneering technology entrepreneur Elon Musk also sees value in taking breaks. When he was interviewed by U.S. Air Force Lieutenant General John Thompson, Musk stated,

*"In my case, I actually want to get the most amount done possible, but if you don't take some breaks then the amount you get done is less. So the reason I take breaks is in order to get more done."*

Given the importance some of the most productive people in history place on taking breaks, it's worth looking into taking short breaks throughout the day. This can help you re-energize yourself, so you can bring a higher level of energy and focused attention to your work.

Consider using a timer that will go off when it's time to take a break or when it's time to return to work after a break. Some traditional types of timers include a Pomodoro kitchen timer, a digital timer, and an alarm you can set on your smartphone or tablet. However, there's a digital block timer that I've personally found to be especially useful.

Digital block timers resemble large dice, and like dice, have six sides. Five of the six sides have a specified number of minutes, which range from one minute to 60 minutes. You can place the time you want to set face up, and then the timer will immediately begin counting down. This makes it very quick and easy to set the timer, and it does not present the same distraction risk you'd have to overcome if you use your smartphone or tablet. However, a downside of using a digital block timer is that it can disturb others when the alarm goes off. Therefore, this type of timer could make more sense for you to use in a home office rather than in an open office environment.

When your timer goes off, you have a split-second decision to make. If, at the moment the alarm goes off, you're in the zone and you want to continue working, feel free to continue doing so until you reach a natural stopping point and you're ready to take a break. However, if you're ready to take a break when your timer goes off, immediately stop working and take a break, even if you're in the middle of typing a sentence. This strategy leverages the Zeigarnik effect, which states that people tend to think about open loops and to want to close them by completing a task. This can help you leverage your subconscious mind to continue working on the task in the back of your mind during your break.

If you complete a task before your timer goes off, immediately take your next break, and then after this break, start your next block of uninterrupted, focused work. During your breaks, consider eating a healthy snack, drinking some water, or going for a walk.

There are two primary approaches to taking breaks. One consists of taking longer breaks infrequently, while the other involves taking more frequent breaks that are shorter. You can experiment with each of these two options for taking breaks and then do what you find works best for you.

When you're determining how long of a break you need, you can start by matching the length of the break to how much you need to re-energize yourself. If you feel great and have a high level of energy, a shorter break could make more sense. In contrast, a longer break could be helpful if you have an especially strong need to replenish your energy and ability to focus.

How you spend your time during breaks can have a significant impact on your productivity when you return to work. For example, if your break involves reading articles on a web site with emotionally charged political topics, you could have a lower level of energy at the end of your break. If your break instead involves taking a walk to get some water and eating some carrot sticks, you'll likely return to your work feeling at least somewhat refreshed.

# Chapter 11 – Email Productivity

## Avoid Using Your Email Inbox as Your To-Do List

On a typical workday, you might spend a significant amount of time addressing the emails in your inbox. Taking this approach can make you feel good throughout the day because it seems like you're getting many things done. However, although you might be getting a large number of things done, you could be spending too much time on items of relatively low importance that serve others' agendas rather than your own highest value work.

Imagine how you'd feel if one of your coworkers stopped by your desk and started writing things down on your to-do list. That specific action would be unusual at most companies. However, it's not uncommon for your coworkers to fill your inbox with emails implicitly asking you to prioritize their requests on your to-do list.

Therefore, when your strategy for deciding what you'll work on is too heavily weighted toward addressing the emails in your inbox, you might feel bad at the end of the day and at the end of the year when you realize you didn't make as much progress on your most important objectives as you hoped you would. Therefore, it's a good idea to avoid using your email inbox as an informal to-do list.

## Use Email Filter Rules

Although some of the emails you receive are more critical than others, by default, they all arrive in the same inbox regardless of their importance. Therefore, to better organize and prioritize your emails, consider using email filter rules to automatically sort the emails you receive into folders that match the level of attention you want to give them. This can help you immediately see important emails right away in your inbox. Meanwhile, less important emails will be immediately filtered and automatically moved into other folders that you can get to later when you have time to batch process them.

For example, if you receive email updates related to current events in your industry, it might be important for you to read them within a few days of receiving them. However, it could be inefficient to read them one by one as they come in. You could set up a filter rule in your email program, such as Gmail or Outlook, that automatically moves these emails into a specific folder immediately as they arrive. This keeps you from seeing these emails in your inbox right away, which could distract you from more important work that would be a better use of your time. Instead, you could hold off on reading these industry email updates until you have time to batch process them a couple of times a week.

### Email Filter Rules Can Help Save You from Repetitive "Reply All" Emails

Have you ever received a barrage of irrelevant "reply all" emails? This typically starts with someone sending an email to a large number of people without blind carbon copying everyone. Then someone who received the email tries to respond only to the sender but accidentally hits "reply all" instead of "reply." Finally, several other people in the email chain purposely hit "reply all" with an ironic request that others stop hitting "reply all" and emailing the whole group.

Rather than wasting your time seeing all the subsequent messages from this "reply all" email chain, you can set up a filter rule in your email program to send the rest of these emails to the trash.

Also, when you send emails to a large distribution list, consider blind carbon copying all the recipients. This prevents the emails you send from turning into the endless "reply all" emails mentioned above.

## Unsubscribe from Extraneous Email Newsletters

I n addition to low priority emails, you probably also receive emails that don't add value to your life. For example, you might have signed up for email updates years ago that are no longer relevant to your current interests and needs. To remove yourself from these email lists, search your emails for the words "unsubscribe" or "remove me" to identify the email newsletters to which you're currently subscribed. Then click the relevant link, which typically says "unsubscribe" at the bottom of the email. Alternatively, you could use a service designed specifically to address this issue, such as unroll.me.

## Check Your Email Strategically Rather Than Haphazardly

I t can be very distracting to see a pop-up notification each time you receive a new email. When you see these notifications, you can lose your focus on the task at hand as your attention shifts to the new email you just received. Therefore, it's a good idea to turn off notifications in your email program to keep incoming emails from distracting you.

Also, it's a good idea to avoid checking your email too frequently. If you regularly reply very quickly to requests you receive via email, you're conditioning others to expect a relatively quick reply from you. This can create unrealistic expectations regarding how fast your responses will be in the future. For example, if you regularly check and reply to your work emails right after you wake up and right before you go to bed, you're implicitly communicating to others that they can expect to reach you at these times in the future. You might think that responding to work emails outside of normal business hours shows others that you're a team player and that you care about being responsive. However, by setting these expectations, others could get much more impatient with you if, on a particular day, you're not able to provide them with an especially rapid response. Also, if it becomes known to others that they can consistently get you to respond quickly to the request they send you via email, they might start to shift more of their own work to you rather than doing the work themselves. That being said, use your judgment and realize that it can still be beneficial to be highly responsive to certain people, such as your boss or an important client.

Therefore, unless it's absolutely necessary, only check your email once every hour or two. This approach can help you shift more of your focus and attention from things that are urgent, but not important, to things that are much more important. It also balances the need to be responsive to critical emails while simultaneously allowing yourself to perform a deeper level of work with limited distractions. When you're not working with emails, keep your email program closed.

It can also be helpful to only check your email when you're able to address the emails you receive. Otherwise, checking your email can result in you unnecessarily wasting your thoughts and energy on emails you receive when it's not even possible for you to take action on them.

When you process new emails in your inbox, start by going through your most recently received emails first. This keeps you from responding to initial emails in a discussion thread where multiple other subsequent responses have already been made.

As you process each new email, immediately determine your next step, which might involve deleting the email if it's not relevant. It's generally a good idea to address an email immediately if you can process it within a few minutes. Also, if an email would take more than a few minutes to address, and it's not time-sensitive, you can move it to a "Get to Later" folder, which you can then batch process at the end of the day.

### Keep Your Emails Short, Clear, and To the Point

T ypically emails that are short, clear, and to the point will receive a response much faster than much longer and more complex emails. Therefore, whether you're sending a new email from scratch, or if you're responding to someone else's email, try to keep your emails to only 3-5 sentences. Also, when you send a shorter email, you give the email recipient fewer things to latch onto, which can reduce the number of questions they send you in return.

There's frequently an inverse correlation between the length of the emails someone sends and their level of experience and seniority. For example, a partner in a consulting firm might write a short, clear, and direct email that says,

*"George – Please send me the deck for our meeting with the client tomorrow. Thanks."*

In contrast, an intern's email to make the same request might sound something like the following.

*"Hi George – I hope you're having a great day. It's been so rainy recently, but I'm really hoping it will be sunny this weekend. I'm reaching out because the big meeting with our new client is taking place tomorrow afternoon, and we need to prepare for it by getting the necessary materials together. Therefore, can you please send me the slide deck for our meeting with the client tomorrow? Please do not hesitate to contact me if you have any questions related to this request. Kind regards, Bartholomew the Intern."*

The second painfully long email reduces the productivity of both the person who wrote it and the unfortunate person who had to read it. Therefore, although it can be a good idea to include some professional niceties in your emails, err on the side of the brevity of the "partner" style of email while avoiding the elaborate "intern" style of email writing.

If you find yourself needing to write more than a few sentences in an email response, or if you're already playing "email tag," consider if it would make more sense to call the person you've been communicating with via email. This can save you time relative to continuing the back-and-forth dialogue with additional emails.

Where possible, only include one main point, question, or request in each email you send. This will allow the person who receives your email to reply quickly instead of waiting until they have answers or solutions to multiple topics. Email recipients typically respond more quickly to shorter emails. This is because it's psychologically easier to get through two short emails compared to one long email.

It's also a good idea to keep the sentences in your emails as short as you can. When your emails consist of shorter sentences and simple but precise words, it's quicker and easier for your email recipients to read and understand your emails. This makes it more likely they'll get back to you more quickly.

Although it's important to keep your emails short and to the point, make sure you include the answers to any questions your recipient is likely to have. This can help you avoid multiple back-and-forth emails.

If someone who reports to you sent you a long and complicated email that would take you a significant amount of time to digest, don't waste your time trying to parse through it. Instead, reach out to the person who sent you the email and ask them to send you a revised version that's shorter and more focused on just the main points they're trying to communicate to you.

### Consider the Impact of When You Send Your Emails

I f it's not already a part of your company's culture to send emails late at night, over the weekend, and during holidays, think twice before you send emails during these times. If you start sending emails significantly outside of normal business hours, this could encourage other people on your team to do the same. Before you know it, your team's culture could shift to one where you're expected to be responsive to requests outside of normal work hours. This could reduce your ability to unplug from your work and rejuvenate yourself, which could reduce your productivity when you return to work.

Many email programs have a feature that allows you to choose a delayed send time, such as the next business day at 9:00 a.m. By refraining from consistently sending emails outside of normal business hours, you can help you and your team maximize your ability to work hard during work hours, and play hard and rest when you're not working.

If you're sending an email that's asking for a favor, consider sending it out on a Friday. People are generally in a better mood on Fridays because the weekend is right around the corner. Therefore, by sending your request on a Friday, the recipient of your email could be more predisposed to giving you what you want.

### Create a VIP Section for the Key People in Your Life

In your personal life, consider using a separate email address for the people closest to you while using a second, more public email address, for everyone else. This enables you to check the email account for your VIPs more often while checking your public email address less frequently.

# Chapter 12 – Smartphone and Tablet Productivity

S martphones and tablets can either help or hinder your productivity, depending on how you use them. In this chapter, we'll go over how you can work with these devices to maximize their usefulness to you, while helping you avoid some of the common pitfalls people often succumb to while using them.

While you're working, consider turning your phone on airplane mode to minimize distractions, such as social media notifications and phone calls. However, in certain limited instances, you might need to have your phone on while you work, such as when you're expecting an important call. Here are some ideas on how to stay productive, even when your smartphone is on.

Don't answer phone calls unless you know the person who's calling you. If you want to level up your productivity even more, you can turn on "do not disturb" on your phone where it will only ring when the same number calls back two times within a few minutes or when certain people call.

Consider deleting unused apps on your smartphone. "App bloat" can occur when you add new apps to your smartphone faster than you delete your existing apps. Having too many apps can make it harder for you to find the apps you want to use. This isn't as much of an issue for apps you use every day, but it can be an issue for apps that you want to use but that you haven't found the time to use yet. The faster you clear out the clutter of apps that you're unlikely to use, the more accessible you'll make the remaining apps that you'd like to start using more frequently in the future.

Consider organizing your smartphone apps based on your objectives. You could start by taking a few minutes to think about which apps you want to use the most. There could be a big difference between the apps you would like to use the most and the apps you've recently been using the most frequently. For an approximation of where you've been spending your time on your phone, you can go into Settings and then Battery to see which of your apps have been using up your smartphone's battery the most. On iPhones, you can also look at the Screen Time data, which will share overall screen time compared to previous days, data points on the apps you use most frequently, and an overview of which of your apps have been sending you the most notifications. This isn't a perfect approach, but it can provide you with a rough estimate of the apps you've been using the most frequently.

Based on how much time you want to spend using each app, consider moving apps to make them more or less accessible to you. For example, if you fly only occasionally, you might still want to keep airline apps on your phone. However, if you don't use these apps very often, you might want airline-related apps to be on the second or third page to the right and not on your primary home screen.

**Productivity Apps**

T here are many smartphone apps you can leverage to increase your productivity. However, here we're going to cover just a couple of the very best ones that I highly recommend.

Evernote is an app that lets you easily take notes in a variety of formats, including text and audio. It also allows you to attach files, such as PDFs and MP3s. You can file these notes into the notebook of your choice, which can help you keep your notes organized. You can access the Evernote app on most smartphones, tablets, and laptops. Also, you can access Evernote with your browser.

Timeular is an app that can help you monitor where you spend your time. Although you can use the app by itself, it's much easier to track your time if you also use the 8-sided Timeular

Tracker dice that work together with this app. To use a Timeular Tracker die, simply go into the app and assign one of your tasks to each of the eight sides. Then, write down the name of the task on each of the eight sides of the die. I recommend using dry erase markers that you could purchase separately to write down your tasks on the die. Then, to track how much time you spend working on a task, simply place the side of the die with the name of that task facing up. The app will then automatically record how much time you spend on each task, down to the minute. As soon as you finish working on a task, place the die back in its holder until you're ready to work on another task. The app automatically generates charts and graphs that summarize where you've been spending your time. If you purchase the premium version of the app, you can export the metrics regarding where you've been spending your time into your choice of a CSV file or an Excel file. This can help you better identify where you're spending more or less of your time than you thought, which can help you better allocate your time.

## Spend Less Time Looking for Your Smartphone

Your smartphone won't help your productivity very much if you regularly spend a significant amount of time looking for it. One solution to overcome this type of challenge is to put your smartphone down in the same place each time you're done using it. This solution is also applicable to other items in your life, such as your car keys and your credit cards.

Another way you can reduce the amount of time you spend looking for your smartphone is to install an app that will let you know where your phone is located. The most popular apps for iPhones and Android devices are the Find My iPhone and the Google Find My Device apps, respectively.

However, smartphones are not the only devices that can be difficult to locate at times. You don't want to show up late for work in the morning because you couldn't find your keys, your work badge, or something else you need. Therefore, consider using a Bluetooth tracker device, such as Tile or Ping, which can help you more quickly find the things you need without having to spend a significant amount of time looking for them. You can then use the related app on your phone, such as the Tile app, to "ring" the Tile Bluetooth tracking device that is attached to the item that is missing.

# Chapter 13 – Make Your Meetings More Productive

M eetings can be a useful tool for collaborating with others to arrive at better decisions, but they can also be a poor use of time if they are approached in the wrong way. In this chapter, we're going to cover how you can make the most out of the time you spend in meetings, as well as ways you can avoid meetings that would not be a good use of your time.

As you move up in an organization into roles of greater responsibility, you might find that meetings begin taking up an increasingly large portion of your workday. Also, even though an increasingly large portion of your day might be allocated to meetings as you move into more senior roles, you'll likely find that you still have a significant amount of work to do outside of these meetings. Therefore, the strategies for approaching meetings that we're going to cover in this chapter will likely only increase in importance for you over time.

### Skip Meetings You Don't Need to Attend

M eetings are most useful for coming up with ideas, working through problems, and making decisions. Although brief status update meetings can be helpful at times, it's often more efficient to share status updates electronically. For example, you can share status updates in a shared spreadsheet on your team's shared drive or in the cloud with a service such as Dropbox or OneDrive. This way, people on your team can quickly provide their own updates and see updates from others at their convenience rather than having to make time for a separate in-person meeting.

When you receive a meeting invitation, before you accept it, first determine whether it makes sense for you to attend. If it looks like the primary purpose of a meeting could be resolved with a quick conversation, consider calling the meeting organizer to resolve the item over the phone. Alternatively, you could ask the meeting organizer to stop by your desk to see if you can address the matter quickly in person rather than setting up a formal meeting.

You could also ask the person who invited you to the meeting what they think you can add to the meeting, and you can also ask for a copy of the meeting agenda. It's common for people to set up meetings without a clear agenda, and meetings without agendas are frequently less productive. If you're not satisfied with the meeting organizer's answers regarding why you need to attend a meeting, take a curious point of view and ask them to tell you more about why they think it would make sense for you to participate in the meeting.

If this additional information clarifies for you why it makes sense for you to attend, then you can plan to go to the meeting. Otherwise, let the meeting organizer know that although you'd like to help out, based on what you've heard so far, it doesn't sound like it would make sense for you to attend the meeting. At that point, you can work to arrive at a reasonable solution, which might involve reviewing meeting notes after the meeting takes place. However, make sure you go out of your way to be respectful to the meeting organizer during these discussions. Otherwise, they could use your absence at the meeting as a free pass to assign you tasks that come up during the meeting that no one else wants to do. If you get in the habit of regularly asking meeting organizers about why you need to attend specific meetings, this can help them be more mindful regarding whether they should include you in the meeting.

When you start avoiding unproductive meetings, you might feel a fear of missing out. However, realize that if you were to attend those meetings, you'd be missing out on much more productive uses of your time. If significant developments arise during a meeting, there's a good chance this information will filter down to you anyway, especially if you review the meeting notes. Although you could experience delays in hearing about things shared at meetings you skip, this is outweighed by the value associated with you focusing your time and effort on your highest value tasks.

While some meetings could be a poor use of your time, others could be a great use of your time. For example, at certain meetings, you might have an opportunity to increase your understanding of other areas of your company or your industry, and at other meetings, you might have an opportunity to further develop your professional network. Therefore, although it's a good idea to have a filter on which meetings you'll attend, think twice before skipping meetings unless you don't see any significant benefits from attending.

### Delegate Meetings or Attend Only Selected Parts of Meetings

If you received an invitation to attend a meeting and you think it could make sense for you to go, consider if you could instead delegate the meeting to someone else on your team. For example, if one of your direct reports could likely handle the meeting by themselves, have them go to the meeting to handle any questions that come up, take notes, and then email you an update after the meeting regarding the highlights of what was covered. Make sure the person going to the meeting will refrain from committing your team to significant new responsibilities without checking with you first. This helps you avoid a situation where your representative at a meeting agrees to do something that you wouldn't have agreed to had you been there yourself.

If you can't avoid attending a meeting and the part that's relevant to you is relatively short, consider working with the meeting organizer to see if your part can be covered at the beginning of the meeting or at a specific time. This will allow you to attend only the part of the meeting that is relevant to you. Also, consider working with the meeting host to set up a dial-in number so you can call into the meeting. This allows you to continue getting work done at your desk while other meeting attendees cover items that are less relevant to you.

It's important to be mindful of the cultural norms at your company, so calibrate your approach to calling in to meetings and leaving meetings early. Depending on your company's culture, violating these norms could have a detrimental impact on your career that outweighs the benefits.

## Prepare Adequately for Meetings You Need to Attend

You can add links and files to your calendar to help you better prepare for your upcoming meetings. For example, for some meetings you attend, there could be a specific file, folder, or other content that is relevant to the topic at hand. Consider adding relevant links or files to your calendar at the same time as the meeting. This can help you more quickly access these materials before the meeting so you can refresh yourself on the topic of the meeting. This increased level of meeting preparation can help you increase the productivity of the meetings you attend.

Before you attend a meeting, determine what discussion points or topics will be addressed. If the points being covered could benefit from you doing some work beforehand, be sure to complete the necessary preparations before the meeting. This can help you have a more productive and informed discussion at the meeting.

Especially if you're meeting with others outside of your company, consider if highly confidential information is reasonably likely to be discussed at an upcoming meeting. Once someone from your company blurts out confidential information, it cannot be unsaid. Therefore, as appropriate, consider reiterating to your team members what information is proprietary and should not be discussed openly.

## Be on Time for Meetings

P lan ahead so you can arrive at meetings on time or a few minutes before they start. However, if you're late, don't provide an excuse for why you were late. This is somewhat counterintuitive. You might think that providing a reason why you were late shows respect for others due to the implicit communication that you didn't intend to be late. However, when you provide a reason for being late, this indirectly communicates to others that you feel somewhat justified in having arrived late. It also implies that you might be more likely to continue arriving late in the future because you're pointing to external circumstances that could recur again in the future.

Therefore, in the rare instances when you arrive late to a meeting, consider saying something more direct and to the point such as, "Thanks for waiting" or "Sorry to keep you waiting." This communicates that you didn't intend to be late, and it implicitly acknowledges that you might have inconvenienced others by arriving late. Although this doesn't make you feel as good in the moment, taking responsibility for being late without providing a justification shows others that you can take responsibility and ownership where appropriate.

Occasionally you might find yourself unexpectedly waiting for others to arrive before a meeting can start. Rather than letting this time go to waste, you can get in the habit of bringing things with you to meetings that you could do to be productive during these times. This helps you get your work done while simultaneously decreasing any inconvenience it causes you when someone arrives late to a meeting.

## Clarify the Meeting's Purpose

I f you're still unclear about the purpose of a meeting when it starts, other meeting attendees are likely unclear about its purpose as well. If left unaddressed, this lack of clarity could result in a meeting that goes on much longer than necessary to complete its intended objectives. Therefore, if you're still unclear about the purpose of a meeting when it starts, ask the group for clarity regarding its purpose. This increased clarity can help people stay focused on the topic at hand, which can result in the meeting accomplishing its objectives more quickly.

## Take Excellent Notes During Meetings

I t's common for meeting attendees to take little to no notes, and often the more senior the executive attending a meeting, the fewer the notes that are taken. However, rather than seeing note-taking as a task for the most junior person at the meeting, take personal responsibility for writing down the meeting's most important developments. The three main categories of notes to take at meetings are brief reminders for yourself, important new things you learned, and takeaway tasks you or others agreed to perform. For takeaway tasks, include the specific next steps and the timing by which these tasks need to be completed, if applicable.

There's significant value in paying close attention during a meeting, so you could miss critical parks of a meeting if you take notes that are too extensive. Therefore, take only a few bullet points worth of notes on average for the meetings you attend to strike the right balance between paying close attention and capturing the key takeaways.

If you come up with an important point you'd like to make during a meeting while someone else is talking, consider jotting down a few words to remind yourself of this point. This can help you focus on what others are saying without forgetting what you were going to say.

If, at any point during a meeting, you agree to take responsibility for performing a task, make sure you make a clear note to yourself about this task. Then, after the meeting, incorporate this task into the rest of your workload to make sure you get it done by the agreed-upon completion date.

## Set Up and Run Productive Meetings

I t's important to reassess if a meeting is necessary before you sent out calendar invites. If what you need to address could be handled in a couple of emails or a quick phone call, consider one of those approaches as an alternative. If a meeting is required, don't feel obligated to set the meeting length to a standard time slot, such as half an hour or an hour. Instead, set the meeting length to only the amount of time you believe will be necessary to accomplish the meeting's objectives.

When you send out a meeting invitation, only include people who need to attend rather than adding in a few additional people just in case they might be needed. The more you're respectful of others' time by not inviting them to unnecessary meetings, the better you'll be able to extricate yourself from meetings that don't make sense for you to attend.

Include a clear agenda regarding the purpose of the meeting in the meeting invitation. This agenda doesn't need to be elaborate, and it's okay if it's only a few bullet points. Even if you haven't fleshed out all the details, include as much information as possible regarding what you plan to cover. This helps the other meeting attendees mentally prepare for the meeting before it takes place, including thinking through topics to be discussed in the hours or days leading up to the meeting.

Also, including a clear meeting agenda can increase the likelihood that the right people will attend the meeting. For example, if someone at your company transitioned responsibility for a specific area to someone else, a clear agenda could prompt that person to forward your meeting invitation to the new person who now covers that area. Therefore, including a clear meeting agenda can help you avoid having to set up yet another meeting with the correct attendees.

You don't need to print and hand out paper agendas. Instead, you could connect your laptop to a projector in the meeting room to display the agenda on the screen. This prominent display of the agenda can help keep the meeting on track. If your meeting is taking place virtually, such as through Teams or Zoom, you could start the meeting by sharing your screen and briefly touching on the key items on the agenda.

It's a good idea to go over the purpose of a meeting as soon as it starts. Mention what will be covered and ask the meeting attendees if they would like to add anything else to the agenda. This provides the group with a clear affirmation of what will be covered in the meeting, which can help you and the rest of the attendees stay on track to accomplish the meeting's objectives. As the meeting takes place, stick to the agenda, and gently bring participants back to the agenda topics if they start to go off on unrelated tangents. However, if a new item comes up during the meeting that could be addressed in a minute or two, use your judgment regarding a reasonable amount of flexibility for non-agenda topics.

At the end of the meeting, make sure it's very clear what next steps the meeting attendees need to take based on what transpired at the meeting. Also, make sure it's clear who's responsible for completing these next steps and when that work needs to be completed.

## Cushy Meeting Room Conditions Can Contribute to Unnecessarily Long Meetings

I f a meeting room environment is too comfortable, it can encourage attendees to keep meetings going on for longer than is necessary. Examples of conditions that can lead to unnecessarily long meetings include chairs that are more comfortable than attendees' chairs at their desks and a great view out the meeting room windows. If there is significant activity outside the meeting room windows, it can be distracting. Therefore, consider shutting the blinds in the meeting room to increase the productivity of the meeting.

Think twice before ordering catering for a meeting. Meeting attendees can be distracted by seeing, smelling, or hearing catered food being set up. Also, when meetings are catered, it's not uncommon for the group to take only a brief break as meeting attendees start getting food. Then, it's not uncommon for the meeting to start up again before everyone has obtained their food. This can keep some people from fully participating in the meeting and not paying full attention if they are still getting their food when the meeting resumes. Also, unlike many machines that can operate continuously at the same level of productivity with minimal downtime, humans achieve more when they take breaks periodically. Therefore, there can be value in having the meeting attendees take a short break for lunch together at a location outside of the meeting room. This can give the attendees a needed break that can help them be more productive when the meeting resumes.

There's no need to actively add elements of discomfort to a meeting to help participants stay on track, such as requiring everyone to stand for the whole meeting. However, if you can avoid creating a meeting room environment that's too cushy for the meeting attendees, you can increase the productivity of your meetings.

## Foster Psychological Safety

When you're running a meeting, do what you can to create an environment where everyone respects each other's viewpoints. This includes each person listening to others' thoughts as they speak, people not cutting each other off, and meeting attendees speaking roughly the same amount. For example, you can notice how often each person speaks and then ask people who have not talked much to share their thoughts on a topic where you think their insights could be helpful.

Simply acknowledging the thoughts and opinions voiced by others in a meeting can go a long way toward making the other meeting participants feel heard and valued. For example, it can be helpful to occasionally repeat back what you took away from what you heard. This shows the people attending a meeting that you were putting in the effort to listen to them, and it also allows them to clarify things they didn't clearly communicate the first time. Even if you don't end up using ideas generated by others, it can significantly increase meeting participants' motivation and engagement when they feel that they were truly heard.

The more meeting attendees believe their thoughts and ideas are truly heard by others, the more open-minded they'll be about considering others' differing viewpoints. However, if meeting attendees don't believe others understand what they're trying to say, they could be more likely to dig in their heels and fight to defend their current viewpoint.

Also, you can usually facilitate a more productive meeting if you spend less time talking and more time asking questions to guide the discussion. Great leaders focus more on listening to others and understanding their viewpoints rather than trying to dominate conversations by talking more than is necessary.

It can also be valuable to notice when people at a meeting you're attending express visible signs of being distressed, annoyed, confused, or withdrawn. When you see this type of body language, consider addressing it directly by asking the person what they're thinking to increase the likelihood that they'll voice any concerns they have. It's typically better for concerns to be expressed and addressed where possible. This reduces the likelihood meeting attendees would leave the meeting with significant unresolved concerns, which could lead to them covertly sabotaging proposals after they're determined by the group. The more you can ferret out any potential objections to the direction in which the group is moving, the greater the likelihood that the decisions the group makes will be broadly supported.

**Productive Presentations at Meetings**

When you're about to start an important presentation at a meeting, you might feel an increase in your heart rate. Rather than trying to pretend that you feel completely normal, instead, acknowledge what you're experiencing. However, mentally interpret these feelings as excitement to give the presentation rather than an indication that you're nervous.

One of the fastest mental adjustments you can make to improve the quality of your presentation is to shift your focus from yourself to others. Rather than focusing on how others perceive you and how they'll judge your overall performance, instead focus on how your presentation can help people in the audience. If nothing else, you can imagine that the people in your audience are hoping you'll give a great presentation because they don't want to waste their time. Overall, shift your focus away from what others are thinking about you and instead focus on giving your audience the best possible experience.

## Persuade Others Productively

I f a significant part of your role in an upcoming meeting involves persuading others, identify potential objections your audience might raise so you can prepare robust answers to them.

To the extent possible, clearly demonstrate to your audience why the action you're recommending is in their own best interest. However, make sure that you also touch on the drawbacks to what you're recommending. This helps build trust with your audience that you're giving them a fair description of the full picture rather than only selectively choosing to share with them the points in favor of what you're recommending.

Also, it's important to show your audience how not taking the action you're recommending would be a more significant risk and could result in more hardship for them compared to the relatively small risk of taking the actions you're asking them to take.

## How to Have a More Productive Question and Answer Session at the End of Your Presentation

W hile you're giving a presentation at a meeting, your audience is in listening mode where they're analyzing and learning from what you share with them. Therefore, if you suddenly end your presentation and ask if there are any questions, you might see only a few hands go up, if any. This is because it can take time for your audience to shift from listening mode to active dialogue mode where they're participating in the discussion.

One way to address this is to ask your audience questions throughout your presentation. This will keep your audience engaged and out of pure listening mode throughout your presentation. Another way to have a more engaged audience during the question and answer session is to mention to your audience that you're going to ask for questions when you're done presenting. This way, they can come up with questions as you speak. As they work to come up with questions, they might pay closer attention to what you're saying. A good time to mention that you're going to ask for questions is a few minutes before the end of your presentation, but you could also mention this at the beginning or in the middle of your presentation.

## Have More Productive Meetings to Brainstorm Ideas

If the purpose of a meeting is exclusively to brainstorm ideas, provide as much clarity as possible to the meeting attendees regarding which problems you are and are not trying to solve. The more the ultimate end goal is clearly understood by those generating the ideas, the more likely the ideas will be useful. Make it clear that, at least initially, the objective is to identify as many useful, practical, and actionable ideas as possible rather than trying to decide which ideas are the best.

When you're part of a team coming up with ideas, it can be more effective for each team member to come up with ideas on their own first before joining a group discussion. This way, each person will have an opportunity to develop unique ideas that are not influenced by others' thoughts. Also, you could have one person collect and combine the ideas generated by team members before the meeting with no attribution regarding who came up with which ideas. This can make people feel more comfortable offering more creative ideas, given that the broader group will not know who came up with each idea.

When people of different levels of seniority are part of a brainstorming meeting, allow the more junior people to share their thoughts first, and then have those higher up in the organization share their thoughts last. This can help foster a more open discussion regarding what more junior people in the company truly think. Otherwise, if the more senior members of the group share their ideas and make their preferences known too early, this can discourage lower-ranking team members from sharing any thoughts that might conflict with what more senior people in the organization are thinking.

As the group shares ideas, write them down where everyone can see them, such as on a whiteboard or easel. Wait until the group has finished generating ideas before you start analyzing them and removing some from consideration. When your group has finished generating ideas, but before you start critiquing them, ask the group to have an open mind about what ideas could potentially work. This can reduce the extent to which people at the meeting will try to find low-hanging fruit by discrediting ideas that are off the beaten path. This more open-minded approach can allow for more ideas, as well as ideas that are more creative.

# Chapter 14 – Increase the Productivity of Your Projects

### Clearly Identify What Success Would Look Like

At the very beginning of a project, identify what it would look like if the project were to be an overwhelming success. Then you can work backward to identify what would need to happen between the current point in time and the project's target completion date to produce that outcome. This can increase the likelihood that you and your project team will be taking the most direct path to achieve what you want to accomplish.

Identify the project's key milestones, and then ensure there's one person who's ultimately responsible for each step. At each of these periodic milestones, make sure the end users of the project's work are consulted regarding whether the planned deliverables are in line with what they need.

It's not uncommon for the customers of a project to not realize until late in the project that they would like to expand its scope. Better communication with the project's customers can result in these scope expansion requests arising earlier in the project. This is beneficial because the sooner the need for a scoping adjustment is identified, the better you'll be able to address it. Therefore, by periodically checking in with the project's customers throughout the project, you can help your team avoid unnecessary re-work and delays in the completion of the project.

### Avoid Unproductive Project Team Meetings

There's not necessarily a need for you to have a 1-hour status meeting every week with your entire project team if the same content could be covered in an email. For example, if a standing meeting for a project typically involves a thoughtful discussion from various project participants about the strategic direction of the project, it could be valuable to keep these meetings.

However, if the meeting is simply a forum for each person to provide updates to the broader group, consider using an email update format instead. Each person working on the project could email their updates for the week to a point person who would aggregate these updates. That point person could then send out a summary update to the broader project team. Alternatively, each person working on the project could add their updates to a shared spreadsheet stored in the cloud, and project team members could each access the broader team's updates as necessary.

In general, be cautious about setting up and attending large project meetings with many attendees. Frequently, the larger the number of people in attendance at a meeting, the less active a role each person will play in the meeting.

## Avoid Untargeted Mass Emails to the Entire Project Team

When you're working on a project with a large team, it can be helpful to establish a clear project culture that only those people who are necessary should be included on project-related emails. When someone on the project team would like to reach out to others working on the project via email, they should only contact the relevant people instead of sending a group message to the entire project team.

Although this type of approach typically has broad support among project team members, some people on the team might express a concern that they could be left out of the loop for certain discussions. One way to balance the need to reduce unnecessary emails with the need to keep people in the loop is to set up a separate email account that is carbon copied on all non-confidential emails related to the project. This way, if someone working on the project needs to find out the latest information about a specific aspect of the project, they can search for that term in the project email account to find these emails.

## Identify and Leverage Lessons Learned

As you work on a project, you can identify "lessons learned," which are insights about what worked well and what didn't. One way to identify "lessons learned" is to periodically take notes about which approaches you took that were especially effective or ineffective. This can help you repeat the effective approaches, and avoid the ineffective approaches, in your future projects.

At the end of each of your significant projects, you can work with your project team to identify "lessons learned." This can help the team to continue using some new approaches to getting things done that worked especially well in the most recent project, while simultaneously discontinuing approaches that did not work quite as well. You and your project team could identify this information by discussing your "lessons learned" in a meeting or through an anonymous online survey you could set up with a third-party provider, such as SurveyMonkey. However, if you use an online survey with a third party, make sure you avoid disclosing to these survey providers any proprietary or confidential information that needs to be protected.

After you identify "lessons learned" opportunities for enhancing how you run future projects, determine which items are worth addressing. For these items, come up with a plan for how you and your project team will leverage this information to increase the productivity of your upcoming projects.

## Don't Fall Prey to "Shiny Object Syndrome"

For many people, the start of a new project is much more enjoyable than the middle or the end of a project. However, although it can be very enticing, work consciously to avoid the "shiny object syndrome" associated with the excitement of starting something new.

If you don't make an effort to finish your existing projects, you might find yourself with many ongoing projects at the same time.

The more open items you have across your ongoing projects, the more likely you'll experience significant task-switching costs, which can lower your productivity.

Therefore, before you start spending too much of your time on a new project, make sure you're spending an adequate amount of time to wrap up your existing projects.

# Chapter 15 – How to Be More Productive in Your Interactions with Others

### Identify and Take Action on What Motivates Each of Your Team Members

If you can increase your team members' motivation, you can boost their work output considerably. This can help your team more consistently produce higher quality work in a shorter amount of time.

By tailoring your approach to motivating your team members to each person's unique motivations, you can be more effective in motivating them. This is because different people are motivated by different things. For example, while some people are primarily concerned with obtaining a better work-life balance, others are much more concerned with how they can take on more responsibility to accelerate their career progression. Therefore, a good starting point to motivate people on your team is to understand each person's unique needs and desires.

You can do this by asking each person on your team individually what they want the most and what they want the least. The more you understand the nuanced differences in what motivates each of your team members, the better you'll be able to motivate them to accomplish their best possible work.

If you would like to take this process one step further, you can also take the time to deeply understand your team members' broader career and personal growth objectives. Then, do what you can to help your team members achieve these goals. The more the people on your team see you as a strong advocate for their own most important career needs and desires, the more productive they'll be in accomplishing great work for your team.

## Provide Your Team Members With Flexibility in How They Complete Their Work

There is value in adding systemization to your team's processes for a variety of reasons. However, just because you would personally complete a task in a certain way doesn't mean your team members need to take the same approach.

When you talk with one of your team members about a task that needs to be completed, communicate the desired end result, the target due date, and some thoughts on how to complete the task.

In some instances, there might be one specific way that a task needs to be completed. If this is the case for a task you're delegating, create a checklist for the task, and make sure your team members are clear regarding which methods of completing the task, if any, are mandatory. This provides clarity to your team members regarding the part of the task where they must use certain established methodologies and the part of the task where they are able to use their own approach to completing it.

However, where possible, allow your team members flexibility in the methods they use for completing a task, which can give them a greater feeling of ownership over their work. This greater sense of ownership can increase your team members' motivation to perform great work for your team.

## Be Authentic and Keep Your Team in the Loop Regarding What is Really Going On

Be transparent with your team members about what is really going on at your company to the extent that you're allowed to do so. If you're always telling people on your team that everything is great, over time, they'll start to discount what you say. If you instead tell your team the true story of how things are going even when challenges arise, the more they'll trust what you say.

For example, if someone on your team leaves the company, it's important to be realistic with your remaining team members about how this team member's departure could increase the overall workload for the people remaining on the team. By being transparent with your team, your team members will feel better knowing that you're aware of their increased workload and that you're working on finding a reasonable solution to address it.

Even though it's important to provide transparency to your team, be optimistic about where your team stands. For example, using the example above, you could emphasize that the remaining team members will now be able to benefit from increased experience working in other areas.

In certain rare instances, it's not possible to be fully open with team members, such as when you're privy to highly confidential information that cannot be shared. However, let this be more the exception than the rule, and be as transparent with your team as you can be.

**Make it clear to Your Team Members That You Value Their Thoughts and Ideas**

By listening carefully to your team members' thoughts and ideas, you can help them feel more valued and engaged, which in turn can provide additional motivation that will increase their productivity.

Encourage your team members to share any ideas they have, and be supportive of their ideas where possible. The more your team members see you as someone who values their ideas, the more motivated they'll be to work hard and to prioritize the tasks you give them to complete.

However, at times your team members might present you with ideas that don't make sense to pursue. When this happens, at least provide them with the courtesy of explaining why it doesn't make sense to take action on these ideas right away. However, even if you don't use an idea generated by someone on your team, your team members will feel more respected if they believe they can count on you to seriously consider their input.

## Use the Feel, Felt, Found Approach to Increase Your Ability to Change Others' Minds

T he feel, felt, found approach involves letting the other person know you understand how they feel, that you also felt a similar way initially, but that after looking at things from a different perspective, you changed your point of view. This approach can increase your ability to get other people to change their minds.

For example, let's say you're trying to convince someone on your team that multitasking typically results in a decrease in productivity. You could start by letting the person know that you understand how they feel because it seems somewhat intuitive that you could accomplish more by making progress on multiple fronts at the same time. You could then let the person know that in the past, you felt a similar way because you thought that you could get more done in less time with multitasking. Then you could let the person know that one day you came across an article that talked about how multitasking can result in a lower level of productivity. At first, you resisted this idea, but as you continued to read further, you noticed that the article made some valid points. Therefore, based on this new information, you can let the person know that you found that in reality, multitasking typically results in a decrease in your level of productivity.

Using the feel, felt, found approach takes more time and effort than it does to simply share your viewpoint with the other person. However, this effort can pay significant dividends. Overall, the more you can get the other person to see that you're right without them having to explicitly admit that they were wrong, the more receptive they'll be to change their mind and agree with your perspective.

## Clearly Acknowledge When Your Team's Work Will Not be Used

S ometimes your team's objectives will change due to unforeseen circumstances. When this happens, you might need to let one of your team members know that some of the work they performed will not be used, which could be demotivating to them. There are a few ways you can mitigate the impact this could have on your team's productivity.

As soon as you realize that a significant amount of a team member's work will not be used, let them know. Provide additional context into what changed, and include an explanation for why you're not going to use the work they performed. Answer any questions they might have, and listen to any frustrations they might express. If applicable, you could mention any silver linings you see in the situation. For example, the team member who did this task might have developed new capabilities through performing this work. Also, your team might be able to leverage at least part of the work performed in a future project.

Consider if it makes sense to change the way you determine and delegate your team's workload to keep this from happening again, and if you make any such changes, share this information with the team member whose work is not going to be used. Even if all you do is acknowledge the frustration the team member might feel about this situation, you can help your team member get over this temporary setback and help them remain optimistic and motivated going forward.

### Be More Productive in Persuading Others by Featuring the Flaws in Your Arguments

W hen you're trying to persuade others, you might be tempted to present only the data points that support your point of view while leaving out anything that would contradict what you're recommending. This temptation can be especially strong when you feel very confident that your recommendation is clearly the best approach. However, if you don't discuss any drawbacks to your suggested approach, your audience could be reluctant to go along with what you're recommending due to a gut reaction that they're not hearing the whole story.

In many cases, it's likely your audience would identify most, if not all, of the significant drawbacks in your recommendation even without you mentioning them. However, when you share the flaws first before your audience identifies them on their own, you take the wind out of the sails of people who might have otherwise been critical of your ideas. When someone in your audience repeats back potential concerns that you already voiced, this doesn't carry the same weight as it would if the same person was the first to express this potential concern. By mentioning some of the key drawbacks to what you're recommending, you demonstrate to your audience that even though you're aware of those flaws, you still support your recommended course of action.

Therefore, if you clearly feature the flaws in your recommendation, your audience will feel more informed and empowered to make a decision because they'll feel like they've heard both sides of the argument. Also, you'll enhance your credibility by showing your audience that you're able to understand and fairly present the positive and negative aspects of what you're recommending.

However, even though it can be useful to share both the positives and the negatives of pursuing your recommended course of action, it's important to be very clear where you stand. You don't want to make it sound as if you considered both the positives and the negatives, but you're not quite sure what to do. Instead, in addition to presenting the most significant benefits and disadvantages of what you're recommending, make it very clear what you recommend.

### Consider Using the "Foot in the Door" or the "Door in the Face" Techniques to Get What You Want

My best friend in college double majored in Management and Marketing, and one day I asked him to share with me the best persuasion technique he learned in his marketing classes. He responded by sharing with me the "foot in the door" technique and its counterpart, the "door in the face" technique. Where appropriate, you can use one of these approaches to increase the likelihood you'll be able to ultimately get what you want from an interaction with someone else.

The "foot in the door" technique involves asking someone to fulfill a relatively small request for you, which can make them more predisposed to agreeing to a much larger request from you shortly thereafter. This leverages the "consistency" principle from Robert Cialdini's excellent book, "Influence." The person who agrees to accommodate your request for a small favor is more likely to agree to a larger request from you in an attempt to be "consistent" with their past behavior.

One of the most famous examples of the "foot in the door" technique was illustrated by one of America's Founding Fathers, Benjamin Franklin. Franklin asked one of his enemies if he could borrow a rare book from his personal library. The enemy, flattered by this request, immediately sent this book to Franklin. By doing a small favor for Franklin, this enemy became much more predisposed to helping Franklin on other tasks.

The "door in the face" technique involves asking someone for a very significant favor that generally results in them quickly denying your request. When you use this technique, you don't have any intention of getting the person to say "yes" to your first ask, but if they do say "yes," then it's just a nice bonus. After the person denies your initial request, follow up by asking for a much smaller request that appears relatively insignificant by comparison. After denying your first request, the person is generally more likely to say "yes" to the second request.

## Let Your Team Members Know Your Expectations

If your team members don't know what you want them to focus on, they might spend their time and effort on work that you consider to be less valuable. Therefore, provide clear guidance regarding what aspects of your team's work that you care about the most. Specifically, let them know what they would need to focus on doing exceptionally well for you to view them as high performers in their current role.

The better the people on your team understand what metrics you use to measure their performance, the better they'll be able to differentiate between what's more important and what's less significant. This clarity also allows your team members to better focus their efforts on the areas that are the most important for your team's long-term success.

## Encourage the Quick Escalation of Potentially Significant Problems

The sooner you're aware of a potentially significant problem, the better you'll be able to adequately address it before it grows into a much bigger issue. However, it's relatively common for people to avoid escalating bad news due to a fear that the recipient will "shoot the messenger" and have a harsh reaction, even if the messenger had no role in causing the problem. If you lash out at people who provide you with bad news, people will be less likely to share bad news with you, which could lead to you being caught off guard by problems that no one has the guts to tell you about. Frequently problems left unaddressed will only get worse over time. Therefore, it's important to avoid reacting harshly when people on your team present you with potentially significant problems.

One way to avoid reacting harshly to someone who shares a potentially significant problem with you is to separate how you'll address the immediate situation from how you'll take action to keep this type of problem from happening again. For example, if a potentially significant problem arises because of yet another failure of a vendor to meet the terms of its service level agreement with your company, first focus on what you can do to overcome the immediate problem of the vendor failure. Also, simultaneously make a note to yourself to address the deeper underlying issues at a later point in time once the dust has cleared and the immediate problem is solved. This way, you can immediately shift your focus to addressing how to overcome the current problem while saving for later any remedial actions you'll take to keep similar issues from happening again in the future.

In addition to encouraging people on your team to escalate potentially significant problems to you quickly, it's a good idea to ask that they simultaneously share a few potential solutions at the same time. You can also ask that they let you know what solution they recommend among the ones they share with you. This can help you more quickly identify a reasonable solution to the current problem, and it also helps your team members further develop their own capabilities to solve more problems on their own.

## Praise Others Publicly, but Be Diplomatic with Criticism

I deally, everyone would have a relatively thick skin, but this is not the case. If you make one of your team members look bad in front of others, it can sometimes result in a significant reduction in their level of motivation to do great work for the team. Therefore, avoid criticizing others in public. If there's any constructive feedback you need to share with someone on your team, don't do it where others are present, such as in a team meeting. That being said, it's important to encourage your team members to respectfully challenge each other's ideas within reason to help your team come to the best outcome. Also, encourage your team members to develop a thick skin so that when they receive public criticism from others, they can see it as an opportunity to grow.

When you need to provide constructive criticism to one of your team members, approach it from more of a "coaching" perspective than the perspective of a supervisor condemning the errors of a subordinate. Focus more on the future state regarding what you'd like to see in your team member's behavior going forward, and dwell less on mistakes and errors they made in the past. For example, if someone on your team made some errors in a deliverable they submitted to you, share with them the corrections you made, and provide them with additional guidance and clarity on what you'd expect in the work they submit to you in the future.

When you provide constructive criticism to one of your team members, characterize the undesirable actions as an isolated event, and assume that the team member involved had good intentions even if the end result was not ideal. In contrast, when you provide praise, characterize your team member's desirable actions as being a part of their character. For example, if one of your team members went out of their way to help someone else, characterize your team member as being a helpful person. This helps ingrain the positive behavior into the underlying self-perception of the person on your team who, going forward, will increasingly see themselves as a helpful person. This can help foster the continuation of the positive behavior you want to continue seeing in the future.

Although it can improve your team members' engagement when you provide them with well-deserved praise in private, public recognition can have a more significant impact. For smaller accomplishments, you can publicly praise your team members in a lower profile setting, such as a team meeting. For more notable achievements, you could have one of your company's executives recognize your team member's contribution in a division or company-wide town hall meeting. When you publicly praise an outstanding accomplishment of someone on your team, you also help incentivize the same type of behavior from others that see the person getting praised publicly. When you offer praise, make it as specific as you can, and provide it as quickly as possible after you see an action you want to encourage.

It's typically a good idea to avoid contradicting other people, especially in a public setting. If a person you contradict has thin skin, they might take what you say the wrong way, whether you explicitly state that they're wrong or even if you imply it. If they take what you say as a personal attack, they could be less open to hearing what you have to say. Therefore, if you hear someone say something that's not entirely correct, but that isn't significant, consider letting it go. However, if someone says something incorrect that relates to an important part of a discussion, correct the person but phrase your disagreement as diplomatically as you can.

For example, while listening to someone's presentation, you might identify a key assumption that's incorrect. This could be an assumption that the economy will grow at a 4% annual rate, while you know that most respected economists are instead predicting only 1% annual growth. In this type of situation, it could be worth it to say something in the meeting. In this example, it might seem like it would be more efficient to simply tell the presenter that this data point is wrong. However, if the presenter interprets this as an attack that calls into question their expertise, they might be much less receptive to what you have to say. If you instead take a more diplomatic approach, you could help clarify the correct data point for the group while allowing the presenter to save face. This increases the likelihood the presenter will seriously consider your point of view. In this example, one way you could address the presenter's inaccurate data point would be to say,

*"That would be great if the economy grows at an annual rate of 4%. However, some of the projections I've seen are somewhat less optimistic. Can you please give me a sense of the data points you leveraged to arrive at the assumed annual GDP growth rate of 4%?"*

This type of approach reduces the likelihood that your question would be perceived as an attack, which increases the likelihood the presenter would seriously consider your question rather than trying to dismiss it out of hand.

Also, we're all human, and humans can make mistakes from time to time. Even if you're 99% sure you're right, there's a

1% chance you could be missing something. Therefore, another benefit of not directly contradicting others is that it can help you avoid the embarrassing situation of publicly stating that someone is wrong only to be proven wrong yourself.

## How to Work Productively with People Who Communicate "Indirectly"

I deally, people would communicate directly with you by clearly stating what they're thinking and what they want. However, in the real world, people who have an "indirect" way of speaking often talk with more ambiguity. Indirect people hint around about what's on their mind rather than explicitly stating it. When you find yourself working with someone with this personality type, spend a little more time and effort to communicate with them than you typically would, so you can identify what they're thinking but not directly saying.

For example, your manager might say something such as,

*"Hey, did you see that request we just received?"*

If your boss has an "indirect" type of personality, this could be their way of asking you to prioritize this task and complete it as soon as possible. Therefore, in a situation like this, you could tell your boss you saw the request and that you plan to complete it the following morning. Then ask if this makes sense or if it should be a higher priority. This allows the "indirect" person to clarify what they want, such as a desire for you to prioritize a task right away. This approach can help you better understand the thoughts and expectations of "indirect" people.

## Enhanced Listening Can Help You Have More Productive Conversations with Others

W hen you think you know what someone's going to say next, it can cloud your ability to hear what they're actually saying. Often miscommunication arises when someone focuses too much on their own perspective and not enough on others' perspectives.

In contrast, paying close attention to what someone says and asking them questions to better understand their perspective can put you in a much better position. This can give you valuable information you can leverage in the future to have a much more effective interaction that can benefit both you and the other person.

When you deeply understand where someone else is coming from, it becomes much easier to identify and effectively address any underlying concerns they might have. This can make them much more willing to work with you on any new ideas or initiatives you're trying to implement. Also, the more closely you listen to what someone wants and what they don't want, the better you'll be able to ensure both you and the other person each get what you want out of the interaction.

As you listen closely to others, pay close attention to the specific words they use to describe what they're saying. A person's choice of words can provide you with some insight into what they're thinking. This can include additional insights on their underlying intentions and what they're thinking and feeling during the conversation.

Also, for each person you interact with on a regular basis, notice their typical baseline way of interacting with you and others. Later, when you're listening to them, you can use this baseline information to more easily spot when something is different about them. You can use this difference to gain some additional insight into what they might be thinking or feeling.

For example, a person you regularly interact with might usually be very talkative, energetic, and outgoing. However, one day you might notice that when you bring up a certain topic, all of a sudden, they become quiet and more reserved. Although this is not definitive regarding what's really going on in their mind, you can use this information as an early indication that this could be an especially sensitive topic for this person.

Also, as you listen to what others say, think twice before saying or doing anything that could be perceived as you being judgmental. This is because people who see you act in a judgmental way might not be as open with you going forward.

Making a conscious effort to understand someone else's perspective is easier said than done, and you'll likely need to expend more effort as you start implementing enhanced listening. However, over time it will become more natural for you, and it can help you have more productive conversations with others.

## Learn from Others Who Have Already Obtained Great Results

T here's no shortage of people who are happy to provide you with as much of their opinions and advice as you're willing to take. However, it can be more effective for you to instead focus on taking advice from people who have already obtained the same results you're trying to achieve right now.

For example, you would likely get a better insight into how to achieve something by talking to one person who has already achieved it than you could by talking to several people who are only starting to think through how they might achieve it.

## How to Deal with Trolls and Nitpickers

S ome people prefer to focus on tearing others down rather than building themselves up. These people, who are often referred to as "trolls," typically have only negative things to say rather than offering constructive criticism. Trolls are usually unwilling to do the work necessary to achieve their greatest potential. Therefore, rather than putting in the work necessary to become successful themselves, they find it easier to try to make themselves feel better by focusing their efforts on attacking others.

In addition to trolls, there are also critics out there who are nitpicky about certain things. Nitpickers are different because they instead offer constructive criticism. They might tell you they think your work is terrible, but they simultaneously offer suggestions for improvement that would make your work more acceptable to them.

When you receive criticism, regardless of whether the source appears to be a troll or a nitpicker, assess what is being said on its merits and determine if it makes sense for you to do anything differently in the future based on the criticism you just received. Then move on. That's it.

Focusing too much on the criticism you receive is a waste of your time and energy. Instead, over time train yourself to see any criticism you receive as a gift from others. This gift could indicate that you're achieving so much success that others are feeling jealous of you, or it could mean that someone took the time to offer you constructive criticism to help you improve the quality of your work. Either way, take it as a compliment that others view you highly enough that they took the time to comment on you and your work.

### Encourage Your Team Members to Get Additional Relevant Training

If you supervise others at work, encourage them to improve their skills with relevant training. If you don't currently supervise anyone, then at least make sure you continue to keep your skills up to date, which can help you add more value over time.

Although your company might not have the budget for executive coaching or in-person training events, consider if it would be worth it to make this investment from your own funds. You are likely the most valuable asset you "own," and your day job is likely your primary source of income. Therefore, similar to how companies typically make investments to improve their net income in the future, seriously consider investing a significant amount of your own money in coaching and training to enhance your capabilities. If you build the right skills, you can increase your ability to generate considerably more income.

There are less-expensive options that can still be very effective. A variety of companies offer relatively affordable online training courses, such as LinkedIn Learning, Skillshare, Coursera, and Udemy. In addition to online courses, there are also free or low-cost learning resources, including audiobooks, YouTube videos, and blog posts.

Although lower-cost training options might seem enticing, there's often a tradeoff between the amount of money a training costs and the amount of time and effort required to leverage it to achieve your objectives. For example, you might be able to make much more progress far more quickly with personalized coaching than you could by only watching YouTube videos. Therefore, when you're getting ready to make an investment of time and money into sharpening your skills, remember that you often get what you pay for.

# Chapter 16 – Delegate Work Effectively to Increase Your Productivity

M ost people have never been taught how to delegate work to others. Therefore, it shouldn't come as a surprise that nearly everyone has had at least one bad experience with delegation. However, once you learn some of the best practices for delegation and pitfalls to avoid when you delegate, you'll be better equipped to increase your productivity by transferring more of your work to others.

Some of the most common objections to delegation include the following:
- The upfront costs of time and money to find and train someone to take on a portion of your work,
- The amount of rework necessary when the work someone performs is not up to your standards, and
- The cost to pay someone to do work you could do yourself.

The thought process behind these objections has some validity. It typically takes an upfront investment of time and effort to establish systems that will allow you to delegate a significant amount of your work. Also, if you don't delegate the right type of work in the right way, delegating can backfire and leave you in a worse place than when you started. Therefore, it's not a surprise that people typically don't delegate enough of their work to reach their maximum level of efficiency and effectiveness.

However, effective delegation can significantly increase your productivity. The more tasks you effectively delegate to others, the more time and energy you'll have to tackle your most important tasks. In the next section, we'll cover how you can determine which tasks are the best candidates for delegation.

## How to Determine Which Tasks Make the Most Sense for You to Delegate

A lthough you can increase your productivity by delegating a portion of your workload, delegation doesn't usually make sense for all of your tasks. Part of effective delegation involves identifying which tasks make more sense for you to do yourself and which tasks you should delegate.

Tasks that are better candidates for delegation include the following:
- Tasks that are recurring,
- Tasks that require a low to moderate level of skill,
- Tasks that take a significant amount of your time, and
- Tasks you don't enjoy performing

In contrast, tasks that might not be great candidates for delegation include the following:
- Tasks you perform infrequently,
- Tasks that require such a considerable amount of skill that they would be difficult to delegate, and
- Tasks that don't take up much of your time to perform

If the current approach to performing a task is inefficient and there are significant opportunities to improve it, think twice before delegating it. Instead, it can be more effective to first improve a process before you delegate it to others.

You aren't limited to delegating either 0% or 100% of a task. Instead, you can delegate only a portion of a task if that would lead to the best balance between what would make sense for you to do and what part makes the most sense to delegate.

When you delegate a task that requires access to content that is proprietary or confidential, make sure the person who will perform the task has the appropriate level of authorization to access the necessary material.

## Document a Task before You Delegate It

B efore you delegate a task, create clear documentation on how to perform it as efficiently and effectively as possible. This is especially important for tasks that are recurring, difficult, or complicated. The documentation can come in the form of a checklist or step-by-step instructions that provide clear guidance on how to perform the task.

There are many benefits associated with developing this type of delegation system, and they typically outweigh the related costs to create documentation by a large margin. First, it reduces the amount of time you need to spend explaining how to perform a task. This is especially useful when you delegate a task to someone who will be performing it for the first time. Second, it increases the likelihood the work will be completed correctly the first time without the need for additional rework. Third, this type of delegation system can significantly reduce or eliminate the number of questions you'd need to answer regarding the steps necessary to accomplish the task.

Although it can take some time and effort to develop a delegation system for a task, you don't need to do all the work yourself. If someone on your team is already familiar with how to perform a task, you can have that person put together a step-by-step guide or checklist on how to complete it. To ensure the documentation on how to complete a task is easy to understand and implement, you can provide it to someone on your team who will use it to perform the task for the first time. If any questions come up in the new person's performance of the task using the delegation system, update the delegation system to address those questions.

Once you have clear documentation on how to perform a task, going forward, you'll be able to spend much less of your time explaining to people on your team how to perform the work necessary to complete it. This is especially useful if there are personnel changes on your team. Also, robust documentation can help reduce or eliminate any key person dependencies you might have on your team. Another benefit is that new team members can use these resources to be productive right away rather than needing to receive extensive training before they can start contributing significantly to your team's work.

## Consider Your Team Members' Proficiency in a Task Before You Delegate It

When you delegate work, consider how busy you expect to be in the near future relative to how busy you typically are most of the time. If you anticipate you'll be especially busy in the near future, focus on delegating less complicated tasks to people on your team who are the most proficient at performing them. This reduces the amount of time you'll need to spend answering questions about how to complete tasks, and it can also reduce how much time you'll have to spend correcting mistakes in the final work product.

However, if you expect you'll be less busy than usual over the next several days, consider delegating more challenging tasks to people on your team who are currently less proficient at performing them. Although this can result in you needing to spend more time answering questions and correcting mistakes, this can help enhance the overall capabilities of your team. By increasing the number of people on your team who could complete certain tasks, you'll be better able to spread your team's work across different team members. This can increase your team's morale because more of your team members will be able to make greater contributions to help share the burden of your team's more challenging work. This better-shared workload can reduce the amount of turnover you experience on your team. Another benefit of cross-training your team is that if people leave your team in the future, you'll have more well-rounded people remaining on the team, which will help ensure a smooth transition.

If you delegate work to someone and they come to you with a question or a problem, avoid the temptation to immediately give them the answer or to jump in and perform the work they're having difficulty completing. Instead, consider taking a few minutes to go over with them what their thought process would be to address this specific obstacle. Guide them through the thought process that will lead them to the right answer rather than simply providing the answer to them right away. This helps your team members improve their ability to think through and solve new and difficult problems on their own. This also reduces your team members' incentive to seek your help with a question or problem they could have figured out on their own.

This approach will take you several more minutes than if you instead give the person the answer right away. However, look at this as an investment of your time in this person's capabilities. The more capable your team members are at solving their own problems, the more productive your team will be. Also, by you taking the time to provide this additional guidance, the team member you're helping is more likely to feel engaged, which can motivate them to want to do better work for the team in the future.

## Provide a Compelling "Why" When You Delegate Tasks

C alibrate the extent of the explanations you provide for why a task needs to be completed to the amount and type of work you're asking someone to perform. If a task you're delegating is relatively quick and simple, provide a relatively quick and simple overview of the compelling reason for doing it. However, for much larger and much less attractive tasks, provide a stronger explanation for why it's especially important that your team completes the task well and on time.

If you'd like to delegate a small task that is easy to perform, delegating the work can be as simple as sending the person an email and asking them to do it. However, for tasks that are larger, more complex, or less attractive to complete, it can be more effective to make sure you also share the broader picture of why the task needs to be performed. The more your team members can see how the work they're performing is personally meaningful for themselves and has a greater purpose, the more motivated they'll be to do great work for you when you delegate work to them.

You could start by describing the most significant benefits that would accrue to your team, your company, and your company's clients if the task is completed well and on time. Then, you could share the most significant negative implications that could result for these stakeholders if the task is not performed well and on time. This additional context can help explain the importance of the task, which could make it more likely that the person performing the related work would take it more seriously.

It's also important to provide more than the compliance aspect of why the task needs to be performed. The surface-level "why" for completing a task might be that it needs to be performed because it's one of your team's internal controls. It might be the case that your company's internal audit department, your external auditors, and your regulators could ding your team if the task is not completed fully and correctly. It's okay to mention this type of data point to the person completing the task. However, keep in mind that this roughly equates to saying that they should do the task because internal auditors, external auditors, and regulators said so. Therefore, feel free to mention the "compliance" aspect regarding why your team needs to perform a certain task, but don't let this be the only rationale you provide.

## Delegate the Task of Delegating Work

C oach people on your team to delegate their own work to increase your team's productivity even further. This could include your team members delegating work to the trash can if it doesn't need to be done with the understanding that they would need to first check with you before discontinuing any of their current job responsibilities. This could also involve your team members delegating some of their work to automation by creating spreadsheets or other process enhancements to improve efficiency.

Enlist the help of your team in automating as much of your team's work as possible. Your team members will typically be closer to the details of your team's processes, so they could be in a better position to identify opportunities to make these processes more efficient. Consider adding an objective in your team members' annual performance reviews that involves identifying opportunities to eliminate unnecessary work, to add automation, and to delegate work where possible.

## Delegate Decision Making Down Closer to the Action

I n most companies, it's common for executives to be inundated by many decisions they need to make. There are some critical decisions where the decision-making power needs to stay with the executive. However, there are also less impactful decisions where someone who reports to them would be fully capable of making the decision instead. By delegating a portion of their decision-making authority, executives can free up time and energy that they can instead focus on other higher-priority matters. Another benefit is that when people closer to the details make more decisions, they can feel more engaged in their work.

Delegating down decision-making authority can also help companies make decisions more quickly. It can take a significant amount of time to get on the calendar of a busy executive to explain a decision that needs to be made that requires the executive's approval. However, this type of delay is largely bypassed when the decision is made closer to the action by someone who is more familiar with the details.

Many people have a reluctance to give up any type of power or control they have, and they therefore cling to any decision-making authority they have. However, by delegating authority to make decisions to your team, you're allowing additional growth and leadership opportunities for people who report to you. This approach also helps you avoid any unnecessary delays if your approval is needed and you're tied up with other things. When you delegate decision-making authority, make sure you also set up a plan to ensure the decisions that are made in the future in this area are reasonable and appropriate.

You can provide the new decision-maker with an overview of the typical thought process you go through when making these types of decisions. For the first couple of iterations, have the new decision maker share with you their planned decisions before they finalize them. This can help you ensure they're on the right track. You can also have the new decision-maker provide you with periodic updates regarding the decisions they make in this area. This can help you verify that they're still on the right track in the decisions they're making.

### Delegate Tasks in Your Personal Life

In addition to delegating tasks at work, it's also a good idea to delegate tasks in your personal life. The more you delegate tasks in your personal life that are time-consuming, frustrating, or otherwise unenjoyable, the more you can use your time outside of work to recharge your batteries. When you make more time outside of work to re-energize yourself, you'll typically return to work with a greater ability to consistently perform higher-quality work, which can help you reach a higher level of productivity.

Frequently, people have a hard time justifying giving other people some of their hard-earned money for something they can do themselves. One of the best ways to overcome this objection is to think about the dollar figure at which you value your time.

If you divide the amount of money you make each year by the number of hours you work each year, you can arrive at a rough approximation of how much money people will pay you for one hour of your time. For example, if you make $50,000 each year and you work 2,000 hours each year, the rough approximation of your hourly rate is $25 per hour. If you make $100,000 each year and work 2,500 hours each year, the rough estimate of your hourly rate is $40 per hour. If there's a task you don't enjoy performing in your personal life and you can pay someone to do it for substantially less than your rough hourly rate, it can make sense for you to delegate the task.

For example, one evening you might want to have Chipotle for dinner. If it would take you 15 minutes to get to the nearest location, 5 minutes to wait in line and get your food, and 15 minutes to get home, in total it would cost you 35 minutes to get this food. However, if you instead use a meal delivery service, such as Door Dash, it might take you only 5 minutes to place your order online and to receive it when it's dropped off at your door. In this example, you'd be saving 30 minutes of your time by using Door Dash rather than picking up the food at Chipotle yourself. Therefore, using a figure from the example above, if your hourly rate is $25 per hour, using Door Dash could make sense for you if the delivery fees are substantially less than $12.50, which is half of your hourly rate. If you earn money at a higher rate per hour, then it would be an even better deal for you to outsource this task.

Although it's a good idea to be on the lookout for time-consuming and unenjoyable tasks you can delegate in your personal life, it's also a good idea to continue performing activities you enjoy. For example, if you enjoy cooking, there's no need to stop making your own meals. Instead, the point is to transfer to other people tasks that are less enjoyable and less meaningful to you, so you can spend more of your time on things you value.

# Conclusion

As you now know, there are many ways you can supercharge your productivity by working more effectively on the right things. However, only knowing about these techniques is not enough. You must take action to implement them.

There are typically multiple solutions to any productivity challenge, and I encourage you to try different approaches to see what works best for you. To get started, commit to taking action on a few insights you gleaned from this book that you feel could make the biggest impact on your daily life, and come up with a plan to execute them.

Implementing these productivity techniques will likely require your conscious thought at first. However, over time as you build them into your routine, they will start to come naturally without you having to put in much effort to continue doing them.

Made in the USA
Columbia, SC
16 November 2020

24713280R00080